SEAFOOD LOVER'S FLORIDA

Restaurants, Markets,
Recipes & Traditions

Bruce Hunt

Globe
Pequot

Guilford, Connecticut

To my mother, Gerry Hunt, and to my grandnephew, Gabriel Hunt, spanning four generations of the Hunt family.

Globe Pequot

An imprint of Rowman & Littlefield

Distributed by NATIONAL BOOK NETWORK

Copyright © 2017 by Rowman & Littlefield

Photographs © Bruce Hunt unless otherwise noted.

British Library Cataloguing in Publication Information Available

Library of Congress Cataloging-in-Publication Data Available

ISBN 978-1-4930-1929-8 (paperback)
ISBN 978-1-4930-1930-4 (ebook)

♾™ The paper used in this publication meets the minimum requirements of American National Standard for Information Sciences—Permanence of Paper for Printed Library Materials, ANSI/NISO Z39.48-1992.

All the information in this guidebook is subject to change. We recommend that you call ahead to obtain current information before traveling.

Contents

Introduction

You are never far from fresh seafood in Florida. With the Gulf of Mexico on one side and the Atlantic Ocean on the other, the most landlocked spot in Florida is still less than 90 miles from the sea. With 1,200 miles of sea coastline, Florida ranks second only to Alaska in coastline length. Add to that our inland water: Florida has more than 30,000 lakes covering 4,400 square miles, and 11,000 linear miles of rivers and streams. The largest lake, Okeechobee, covers 730 square miles. The longest river, the St. Johns, travels 273 miles. So it is easy to see why seafood rules on both the Florida restaurant scene and Floridians' home dining tables. There's nothing like fresh-caught Florida grouper, snapper, or hogfish. Our Gulf pink and deepwater royal red shrimp are the envy of the world. And Florida's spiny lobster, stone crab claws, bay scallops, and Apalachicola oysters are almost sweet enough to qualify as desserts.

In *Seafood Lover's Florida* we will take a journey to seek out and sample the vast variety of choices in Florida's most iconic category of foods, in some of its most iconic places. It's a journey that begins at the state's far-northwest edge and meanders all the way down to its southernmost tip. This book is not just about seafood, it's also about

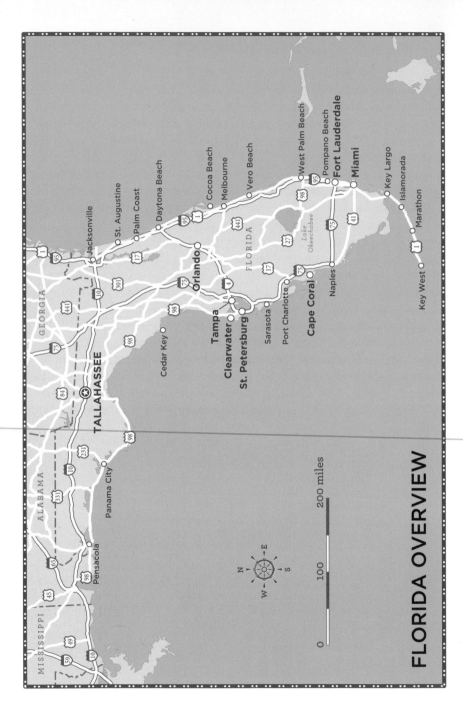

FLORIDA OVERVIEW

seafood "places." For me, the place—the location, ambience, and history—is almost as important as the food. Notice I said "almost" . . . because food always trumps atmosphere. If the food's no good, all the atmosphere in the world won't save it.

I'm no restaurant snob though. I'm actually happiest walking into a joint with a screened porch and fish-cleaning tables out back. I'm particularly keen on hunting down places that are well off the beaten path—local, mom-and-pop dives with "Florida flavor" food. Some of Florida's best seafood comes from these less-pretentious establishments: raw bars, crab shacks, and fish houses. Places like Snook Haven on the Myakka River near Venice, Goodrich Seafood on Mosquito Lagoon in Oak Hill, and Alabama Jack's on a barge next to the Card Sound Bridge in that brackish nether land between Miami and the Keys. The emphasis isn't on haute cuisine here but on *simple* and *fresh*. Many have a close relationship with local fishing fleets, and some even have their own boats, so they are often your best bet for dining on something that was swimming around in the ocean that morning. And here's one of Florida's best seafood-seekers secret tips: Sometimes there are great chefs in these places too.

But *Seafood Lover's Florida* doesn't ignore the "wear a tie and make a reservation" restaurants. Florida has plenty that serve spectacularly good seafood. Okay. I don't really know of any Florida restaurants where you are actually required to wear a tie, but we do have some outstanding upscale joints, and so I've included them too. They include places like Norman's in Orlando, Oystercatchers in Tampa, Bud & Alley's in Seaside, and Louie's Backyard in Key West.

I think most everyone would agree that it's possible to have a great passion for music and yet not be able to play an instrument or carry a tune. I feel like the same might be true for food. I am ardently passionate about good food and yet admittedly I am a lousy cook. But I love food. I love the science behind preparing food, and I am in awe of the genius that it takes to extract enticing variations in flavor. In my opinion the great chefs deserve a place alongside the great composers, and Florida has attracted some of the greatest. Accordingly, you will find here, interspersed among descriptions of 180 restaurants and markets, a few interviews with some of these geniuses, like Harold Russell from Backfin Blue Cafe in Gulfport and Justin Timineri, Official State of Florida Culinary Ambassador. With its great abundance and variety of food, Florida has attracted the most inventive and talented chefs to prepare it.

It's difficult to appreciate how special something is when you've had it your whole life. I grew up on Spanish and Cuban food. To me it wasn't "Latin food." It was just food. I was in college before I figured out that *picadillo* wasn't a Thanksgiving staple everywhere. Florida's history has always been about the collision of cultures. Long before the term "fusion" became part of the modern food-world lexicon, Floridians were creating dishes that blended cultural styles. As a result, Florida-style seafood reflects many influences: Spanish, Cuban, Bahamian, Greek, Puerto Rican, and Italian, to name only a few. But Florida's seafood history dates back even further.

If you go back far enough, you'll find that most food preparation and cooking styles were born out of necessity, not out of an attempt to make it tasty. Spices, marinades, and smoking were all originally ways to preserve food (in a time when there was no refrigeration), not to flavor it. These techniques predate the arrival of European explorers but were widely practiced by Florida's original inhabitants. Today some of those same techniques are as popular as ever and are vital components of the art of Florida seafood cooking.

I am looking at a night photograph of Florida taken from an orbiting satellite, vividly displaying the concentration of light, and therefore the population, along the coastlines. But it was this way long before satellites and long before electricity. Throughout human existence we have chosen to settle along coasts, oddly enough right on the fringe of an environment that is so absolutely hostile to us. Why are we so attached to the sea? Perhaps it is because the sea has always been such a generous, seemingly endless supplier of sustenance. And now that attachment is simply in our DNA. I've lived my entire life in coastal Florida. And as much as I love the majesty of mountains and canyons, if I'm away from the coast for too long, I begin to feel claustrophobic.

Those early Florida inhabitants—Calusas, Timucuans, Tocobagans, and the like—were avid consumers of seafood. They hollowed out logs into long canoes to travel along the coast, up rivers, and across lakes to catch fish and collect shellfish. Our craving for seafood has continued to grow ever since, and today we are more passionate about it than ever. My hope is that *Seafood Lover's Florida* will guide you to the freshest, the tastiest, and the best seafood Florida has to offer. So toss it in your glove box and go explore.

•••——————— ••••——————— •••

I spent the better part of the year crisscrossing the state on seafood-research road trips. I ended up with 180 seafood restaurants and markets, but I actually visited over 250. The hard part has been sorting through them and picking out which to include in this guide and which to discard.

I found amazing Florida seafood all over the state, sometimes in the most off-the-beaten-path places like Oak Hill, Ozello, Card Sound, Perdido Key, St. Marks, Cedar Key, and Cross Creek. I also found some towns with such extraordinary concentrations of sensational seafood restaurants that I consider them worthy of being labeled "Florida Seafood Towns": like Key West, Marathon, Apalachicola, Fernandina Beach, Anna Maria Island, St. Petersburg, and my hometown of Tampa.

Over the years I have visited and dined in what I consider many "great food cities," like Charleston, South Carolina; New Orleans; San Francisco; and the grandest food city of them all, Paris. But Florida is an entire "great food state," and seafood is at the top of its list of great foods. All the "great" ingredients intersect here: We are surrounded by water and have access to the freshest and best fish. We are a veritable crossroads of cultures: Cuban, Caribbean, Central and South American, Bahamian, Spanish, Italian, and Greek, and all have influenced our food dramatically. And these ingredients have inspired great Florida chefs like Justin Timineri and

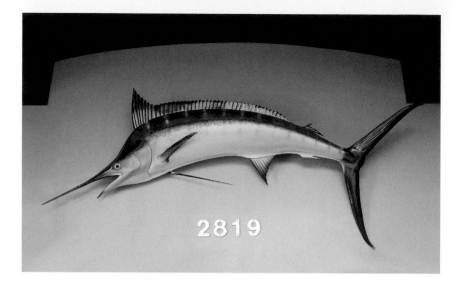

brought other great chefs to Florida from elsewhere, like Emeril Lagasse and Norman Van Aken.

Invariably I am going to be asked what my favorite seafood places were, and I want everyone to understand that I am not being evasive when I say that it is impossible to pick just one, or even a few. Picking "bests" is very subjective. Not only does each individual have varying tastes and therefore opinions, but those opinions can change from day to day depending on what they had for dinner last night. I'm no different. My favorite tends to be the place that served the last good thing I ate, and that opinion can be influenced by the atmosphere, the location, or even whom I dined with. With consideration for those caveats, here are some that are most memorable for me: the Flora-Bama Lounge on Perdido Key, Joe Patti's Seafood Market in Pensacola, Bud & Alley's in Seaside, Tamara's Cafe in Apalachicola, España and Joe's 2nd Street Bistro both in Fernandina Beach, Peck's in Ozello, Becky Jack's in Weeki Wachee, Dockside Dave's in Madeira Beach, Backfin Blue Cafe in Gulfport, the Rod and Reel Pier in Anna Maria, Tide Tables in Cortez, Owen's Fish Camp in Sarasota, Goodrich Seafood in Oak Hill, Norman's in Orlando, Peace River Seafood in Punta Gorda, Doc Ford's on Sanibel, Avenue 5 in Naples, Joe's Stone Crab in Miami Beach, Mrs. Mac's Kitchen in Key Largo, Keys Fisheries in Marathon, and Louie's Backyard, Seven Fish, and Blue Heaven, all in Key West. That list could change tomorrow.

During my travels researching this book, I repeatedly observed some things that have led me to a few random, and perhaps trivial, conclusions:

1) Seafood always tastes better when you're overlooking the water: an ocean, a lake, or a river.

2) You can definitely taste the difference between fresh fish and frozen. With all the great fresh seafood restaurants in Florida, why would anyone bother with one that serves frozen?

3) Some of the best seafood can be found at some of the least-likely places, e.g., rural, off the beaten path, not well advertised, and sometimes downright divey looking. So don't judge a seafood joint by its uninviting exterior, or by its poorly designed website (or lack of one), or by its parking lot filled mostly with rusty pickup trucks.

4) There seems to be an overabundance of tropical-island-themed seafood restaurants in Florida. You'll recognize the look: *Gilligan's Island* decor: thatched roof, palm-frond ceiling fans, shark hanging on the wall with some poor guy's leg sticking out of its mouth, and a sign out front with either a grinning cartoon toucan, sea turtle, pelican, shark, or pirate, and of course a Jimmy Buffet soundtrack in the background. Mind you, this is not a complaint, just an observation.

How to Use This Guide

Not only is Florida culturally diverse, it is also topographically. With both in mind, I have divided *Seafood Lover's Florida* into six regions: Northwest (the "Panhandle" and the "Big Bend"), Northeast, Central West, Central East, Southwest, and Southeast (including the "Keys").

I've compiled a list of 180 restaurants, raw bars, and fish markets. Yes, I visited them all, and I'll tell you what I discovered at each one. You will also find an assortment of sidebars: some fun Florida seafood facts, how-to information, and interviews. Then there is a list of Florida seafood festivals, from Steinhatchee's Scallopalooza to Sopchoppy's Worm Gruntin' Festival. And lastly, you will find recipes, collected from great chefs and great friends, plus one of my own. For these the theme is simple dishes that are easy to prepare at home.

Three generations of my family have called Florida home. My grandparents moved here in the 1920s, and I've lived here my whole life. Because of that, when I write about Florida, it is from a very personal perspective. So when I voice a strong opinion, or it seems like I'm ordering oysters on the half shell at half the restaurants I visited, please take it with a grain of salt (preferably sea salt). I know that not everybody loves raw oysters, but I do!

•••————————•••••————————•••

Northwest

Florida's "Panhandle" rests between the northern coast of the Gulf of Mexico and the Alabama and Georgia state lines. It has far more in common with those two states, both geologically and culturally, than it does with the rest of Florida. Locals fondly refer to their coast as the "Redneck Riviera." To the north, up closer to Alabama and Georgia, rolling hills, river crossings, and pasture land dominate the landscape. Meandering two-lane roads navigate elevation changes and connect the dots between isolated small towns. Along the coast, beach towns sit among windblown sand dunes and overlook pristine glistening white beaches with sand made of quartz washed down from Appalachian mountains over thousands of years.

Panhandle cuisine is significantly influenced by Alabama and Georgia Southern-comfort-food ingredients and preparation, as well as New Orleans Creole and Cajun styles of cooking. It's worth noting that Emeril Lagasse, arguably New Orleans's most famous chef, moved to Destin on the Florida Panhandle coast in 2012. Traveling east, the Redneck Riviera gives way to the "Forgotten Coast" at the elbow in the Panhandle, where one of Florida's most significant seafood towns, Apalachicola, "the Oyster Capital," sits at the mouth of the Apalachicola River. Continuing east and bending south along the "Big Bend Coast" are additional seafood-reliant towns: St. Marks, Steinhatchee, and Cedar Key. This entire northwest region wraps around the northern end of the Gulf of Mexico, arguably Florida's seafood breadbasket.

●•● ———— •◆◆• ———— •●

Apalachicola

Apalachicola Seafood Grill, 100 Market Street, Apalachicola 32320; (850) 653-9510. The town's oldest restaurant, the Apalachicola Seafood Grill opened in 1903. A vintage sign out front advertises the "World's Largest Fried Fish Sandwich." That would be their half-pound Alaskan haddock sandwich. A weekly changing menu favors Southern and New Orleans dishes. My Cajun red beans and rice with blackened fish, shrimp, scallops, andouille sausage, and cornbread matched the best I've had in the French Quarter. They also have oyster or shrimp po'boys and crab cake or salmon sandwiches. For dinner they have a full assortment of platters: shrimp, grouper, scallops, crab cakes, and of course oysters.

Boss Oyster, 125 Water Street, Apalachicola 32320; (850) 653-9364; bossoyster.com. New Jersey transplants Larry and Caroline Maddren opened Boss Oyster in 1991 in the riverfront location that it shares with the Apalachicola River Inn. They serve oysters prepared 17 different ways, 18

if you include just plain "chilled on the half shell." Or you can design your own customized oyster dish via a "Customize an Oyster" submittal page on the website.

Owl Cafe, 15 Avenue D, Apalachicola 32320; (850) 653-9888; owlcafeflorida.com. The Owl Cafe sits 1 block from Apalachicola's waterfront, within sight of the shrimp boats docked along the river. Greek brothers John and Constantine Nichols opened their restaurant and boarding house here in 1908 to serve dockworkers. Back then the specialty of the house was "Whole Loaf," a hollowed-out loaf of fresh-baked bread filled with oysters.

Today the Owl Cafe offers an assortment of entrees like black grouper fillet sautéed with artichoke hearts and roasted garlic, and shrimp, chicken, and sausage jambalaya. My special-of-the-day Thai Whole Snapper was both a spectacle to see and to consume. They prepared it scored and dredged in rice flour, then pan-fried, and doused with a sweet Thai teriyaki sauce. Of course they also serve local Apalachicola Bay oysters on the half shell or fried, and while Whole Loaf hasn't been on the menu for decades, the Owl Cafe does bake their own marvelous bread and serve it with every meal. They also do brunch on Saturday and Sunday, with some tantalizing specialties like sautéed shrimp-and-grits, sausage-and-shrimp jambalaya, and pork-and-gator sausage Creole with grits.

Up the Creek Raw Bar, 313 Water Street, Apalachicola 32320; (850) 653-2525; upthecreekrawbar.com. You have to follow the riverfront road upstream a few blocks to get "up the creek," but you will find some of Apalachicola's best seafood here. Patrons have a serene view of the Scipio Creek Channel tributary off the Apalachicola River from a second-floor

Apalachicola's Seafood Heritage

Perhaps no other Florida town has a history so deeply rooted in seafood as Apalachicola. Two of Apalachicola's seafood restaurants, Apalachicola Seafood Grill and the Owl Cafe, are well over 100 years old.

The Apalachicola River has always been the town's lifeblood. In the 1820s this was a big cotton-shipping port. From the 1860s to the 1880s, sponge harvesting was big here, until the industry moved to Tarpon Springs. In the late 1880s cypress, oak, and pine milling and shipping revitalized the town. And then in the 1920s, it became the center of Florida's booming seafood industry.

Apalachicola has long been known as Florida's Oyster Capital. Historically, up to 90 percent of Florida's oysters have come from the Apalachicola Bay's fertile waters. The clear, clean freshwater that flows out of the Apalachicola River hits the salty Gulf of Mexico, creating a perfect brackish balance for breeding in the shallow waters of Apalachicola Bay. Apalachicola oysters have a well-deserved reputation for being just a little sweeter, a little tastier.

But over the last decade, their oyster population has been on the decline. To understand why, you have to start way up in the Appalachian Mountains, where snowmelt and rainwater drains and filters over waterfalls and down mountain brooks. Eventually those brooks converge with major rivers like the Chattahoochee, which feeds Lake Lanier, just north of Atlanta. Lake Lanier is one of Atlanta's primary sources of water, and Atlanta's exploding population has been syphoning off more and more of the lake's water, which, downstream, feeds the Apalachicola River. Now the bay's perfect brackish balance has been upset and it can't produce oysters as abundantly as it once did. They still get oysters here, and they're as tasty as ever, but the yield has dwindled steadily for the last 10 years.

Proving its perennial heartiness, Apalachicola has always managed to reinvent itself. In 1983 a guy named Michael Koun, who loved old historic buildings, bought a dilapidated downtown 3-story Victorian hotel called the Gibson Inn and spent 2 years restoring it. Koun's restoration helped kick off a wave of historic renovation that spread throughout the town, turning Apalachicola into a historic-Florida tourism destination.

Still, Apalachicola has worked hard to maintain its status as a working town whose livelihood has, for centuries, been tied to the sea. Today shrimping surpasses oystering as Apalachicola's dominant seafood business. And the town continues to embrace and promote its heritage, drawing visitors to its unique shops and galleries, bed-and-breakfasts, inns, and exceptionally good seafood restaurants in downtown Apalachicola.

screened porch at this unpretentious cafe that opened in 2008. Some of their most popular items are fresh-out-of-the-Gulf peel-and-eat shrimp and a variety of fresh-out-of-the bay oysters on the half shell. Try Oysters Moscow with caviar, or Mediterranean with olives, capers, and garlic, or Southern with collard greens and bacon. I sampled their superb cobia sushi, along with a platter of their spicy heads-on peel-and eat shrimp.

Tamara's Cafe, 71 Market Street, Apalachicola 32320; (850) 653-4111; tamarascafe.com. Tamara Suarez, a former television producer from Caracas, Venezuela, came to Apalachicola in 1998 and opened Tamara's Cafe Floridita on Avenue E to rave reviews. Ten years later Tamara's Cafe moved 2 blocks down the road to Market Street, and Tamara turned over the reins to her daughter Marisa Getter and son-in-law Danny Itzkovitz.

Tamara's Cafe's menu mixes native Venezuelan recipes with Caribbean and Florida dishes. Their pecan-crusted grouper with jalapeño sauce and their paella are popular regular items, but on my last visit I tried a special: pan-fried whole lionfish over black beans and rice with fried plantains. Lionfish is a non-native, invasive species to Florida's reefs that aggressively attacks native fish. The State of Florida has been actively campaigning to encourage catching this colorful but destructive fish. Lionfish is light, flaky, and very flavorful. (For more about the lionfish, see my sidebar: "Alien Invasion in Florida's Waters: Attack of the Lionfish.")

Tamara's serves a special tapas menu on Wednesday night. Expect sensational small dishes like *gambas al ajillo* (shrimp sautéed in garlic), *calamares rebosados* (calamari with tomato sauce), and shrimp and scallop ceviche *Ecuatoriano* (Ecuadorian).

Cedar Key

Big Deck Raw Bar, 331 Dock Street, Cedar Key 32625; (352) 543-9992; facebook .com/Big-Deck-Raw-Bar-Cedar -Key-FL-106158406072753. The Big Deck is actually a not-so-big, open-air, walk-up joint that hangs precariously over the edge of the backwater on Dock Street in Cedar Key. Don't be fooled, however, by the unpretentious decor. Big Deck has (in my opinion) the best grouper sandwich on the island. I get mine grilled, and it comes seasoned with a lemon-pepper topping. Their grouper fillet is always fresh out of the water and hefty enough to completely hide the soft egg-bread bun. They also do shrimp and oyster po'boys, a crab cake sandwich, peel-and-eat shrimp, and naturally steamed Cedar Key clams. Locals

Bryan and Darlene Skarupski, who also own the Market at Cedar Key, opened Big Deck in 2011.

Island Hotel, 373 2nd Street, Cedar Key 32625; (352) 543-5111; islandhotel-cedarkey.com. Cedar Key's oldest structure and most famous landmark, the Island Hotel sits at the east end of 2nd Street, in defiance of fires, floods, hurricanes, and even the Civil War. It was constructed (originally as Parsons and Hale's General Store) in 1859 with oak beam frames and 12-inch-thick, oyster-shell-reinforced tabby walls. When Union troops invaded the town during the Civil War, they burned most of the buildings but left the store standing because they needed it to warehouse supplies and house their troops. Three decades later the infamous 1896 hurricane would flatten most of Cedar Key but leave the store intact.

Developer Simon Feinberg bought the building in 1915 and remodeled it into the Bay Hotel. The second-floor veranda that wraps around two sides of the hotel was added during his tenure. In the years that followed, the hotel changed names and owners frequently. During the Depression one owner tried to burn it down three times for the insurance, but the fire department at that time was just across the street, and they always managed to save it.

When Bessie and Loyal Gibbs bought it in 1946, it had been a rundown brothel for a number of years. They patched it up and renamed it the Island Hotel. Gibby ran the hotel's Neptune Lounge bar and Bessie ran the restaurant. Her culinary skills soon won them popularity and customers.

Today the Island Hotel's dining room is still known for its native Florida seafood dishes, like their baked crab Imperial and their garlic-and-butter Clams Island Hotel over pasta, but it is most famous for its Hearts of Palm Salad, one of Bessie's culinary inventions. Not as famous but just as tasty are their Low Country Shrimp and Grits appetizer and their crab bisque, and they also do a fine fresh-catch piccata.

In 2004 husband and wife Andy and Stanley Bair purchased the hotel and spruced the place up nicely, while still maintaining its rustic old-Florida charm. It's worth mentioning that the Island Hotel is famously haunted (although I've stayed several times and have yet to encounter any ghosts). Be sure to look in to see the tiny Neptune Lounge, one Florida's most quaint and classic bars. The painting of King Neptune hanging behind the bar was painted by Helen Tooker in 1948. That painting, like the hotel, seems to be blessed with multiple lives. It has survived gunshots and hurricanes, even flooding when a 1950 hurricane tore part of the Island Hotel's roof off.

Steamers Clam Bar & Grill, 420 Dock Street, Cedar Key 32625; (352) 543-5142; steamerscedarkey.com. With a spectacular upstairs view out over the Gulf of Mexico, Steamers is a great place to sample local seafood.

Driving Back in Time to Cedar Key

Highway 24, off Highway 19, from Otter Creek to Cedar Key, seems like a road that carries you back in time. At its end you will reach the Gulf of Mexico and see what almost all of coastal Florida looked like a hundred years ago. Cedar Key is the town's name, but it's actually on the island of Way Key, once a way station for sailing vessels to resupply and drop ballast. This was a bustling little port town in the mid- to late 1800s. Florida's first cross-state railroad, the Atlantic to Gulf/ Florida Railroad Company Line, completed in 1861, ran from Fernandina to Cedar Key. Cedar milling was the dominant industry here up until the 1890s. The Faber pencil company had a mill on nearby Atsena Otie Key. But then, in 1896, a hurricane decimated the region. The pencil industry left, and Cedar Key regressed to a sleepy fishing village. Eighty years later it began to reinvent itself as an artist enclave, and today it is still a sleepy but scenic place.

Their Low Country Boil, with shrimp, crabs, mussels, corn, potatoes, and of course clams, is their signature menu item, and they also do fried oysters, soft-shell crab, fish-and-chips (with haddock), and a grilled portobello mushroom with blue crab all wrapped in a pastry.

Tony's Seafood Restaurant, 597 2nd Street, Cedar Key 32625; (352) 543-9143; tonyschowder.com. Eric Jungklaus opened Tony's Seafood (named for his brother, who helped him build the restaurant) in 2005. It occupies the lower floor of the historic circa-1880s Hale Building at the west end of Cedar Key's main street, 2nd Street. Eric's claim to fame is his award-winning clam chowder. It won the prestigious Newport, Rhode Island, Annual Great Chowder Cook-Off 3 years in a row. They finally asked him to retire from entry in the contest so others would have a chance. With an emphasis on fresh and local, Tony's serves some scrumptious dishes like grilled teriyaki shrimp, Tuscan Shrimp Italiano, the local requisite steamed clams, and of course award-winning clam chowder. With room for just 54 customers, you may have to wait a bit to get a seat, but it will be worth it. By the way, Tony's now sells their award-winning clam chowder in cans. You can get it directly from them or find it at most Florida grocery stores. I buy it at my local Publix.

Southern Cross Sea Farms

12170 State Road 24, Cedar Key 32625; (352) 543-5980;
clambiz.com

In 1994 Florida voters passed a constitutional amendment that limited the size of fishing nets to 500 square feet, effectively instituting a commercial net-fishing ban as of 1995. Multi-generation fishing families, put out of business by the new law, began to look for alternative ways to make their living in the industry they knew best: seafood.

One result was the rise of aquaculture, or seafood farming. The fertile shellfish grounds in the mud-bottom bay waters around Cedar Key made this an ideal location to begin clam farming. Today 90 percent of Florida's clams come from these waters.

One of Cedar Key's largest farmers is Southern Cross Sea Farms. On Friday afternoons they allow visitors to tour their facility. Co-owner Jon Gill was our guide on my visit. Jon walked us through the operation's entire process, from beginning to end. Southern Cross Sea Farms is vertically integrated. They spawn, hatch, raise, and grow their clams, then sell them fully grown to wholesalers, markets, and some directly to retail restaurants. They also sell hatchlings, ready to be "planted," to other clam farmers. The process begins in their spawning tanks, where they circulate estuary water with phytoplankton "food." One clam can produce as many as 2,000 eggs. The young seedling clams that result are then moved to the "nursery" outdoor tanks where they can grow. The spawning and nursery phase takes about 6 months, after which the young clams are placed in large mesh bags and planted in the bay mudflats, in 2-acre plots leased from the state. They spend approximately a year and a half maturing in the bay (with one interim transition to larger-hole mesh bags) and then are packaged and sold. Southern Cross overnight air-ships their clams all around the country. Most of those that they ship are medium-size, the most popular size, according to Jon.

Clam aquaculture is a very ecologically sound and envi-
ronmentally clean business. Since farmed clams grow in their
natural habitat and are fed and raised only with natural pro-
cesses and water from the bay, there is essentially no impact
on the environment. In fact, clams are natural filterers and
actually clean the water they live in. Now Southern Cross is
testing the waters with oyster farming.

Destin

Dewey Destin's Seafood Restaurant, 9 Calhoun Avenue, Destin 32541; (850) 837-7575. **Dewey Destin's Seafood Restaurant,** 202 Harbor Boulevard, Destin 32541; (850) 837-7525; destinseafood.com.

Dewey Destin's Seafood Restaurant didn't take their name from the town. It was the other way around. The town is named for Dewey's great-great-grandfather, Leonard Destin, who settled here in 1835 and built his family's commercial seafood business here. They called it East Pass then, but in 1904 the local postmaster submitted the name change "Destin" to the United States Postal Service. Four generations later Dewey Destin opened Dewey Destin's Seafood Restaurant at the original family dock/seafood market location on the Choctawhatchee Bay side of Destin. Not long after, he opened their second location on the Destin Harbor Inlet. Steamed local-caught peel-and-eat, by-the-pound shrimp is their specialty, but they also have a variety of platters—fried, steamed, and grilled. In fried platters you can get soft-shell crab, shrimp, scallops, oysters, or crab cakes. Steamed platters include shrimp, scallops, snow crab, and grouper Parmesan. And they will grill their fresh catch of the day, shrimp, or yellowfin tuna. You can also order anything they offer in a platter as a sandwich.

Sexton's Seafood Market, 601 Harbor Boulevard, Destin 32541; (850) 837-3040; sextonsseafoodmarket.com. Sexton's Seafood Market has been providing fresh seafood to Destin since the early 1980s. The giant shrimp on their sign out front hints that this is a specialty. And there's a wide variety of shrimp: Royal reds, pinks, whites, and rock shrimp dominated the counter when I visited. They also had an impressive selection of snapper—red, mangrove, and white—plus cobia, triggerfish, and pompano. Sexton's also makes its own tuna spreads, bisques, and gumbos.

Take the (Walton County) Road Less Traveled

Highway 98 is the Panhandle's main coastal east–west throughway. However, there is a worthwhile detour just east of Destin. Walton County Road 30A dips down and winds along an idyllic coastline for 20 miles, where it follows a stretch of beach consistently rated among the most beautiful in the United States. Road 30A passes through the beachfront communities of Blue Mountain, Grayton, WaterColor, Seaside, Seagrove, and Rosemary. Grayton Beach is the oldest, first homesteaded by Army Major Charles Gray in 1885 and then officially founded as Grayton Beach 5 years later. The small Florida Cracker stick cottages that residents built here back then are now the inspiration for the coastal architecture that has become so popular in the nearby resort villages of Seaside and WaterColor.

Grayton Beach

Fish Out of Water, WaterColor Resort, 34 Goldenrod Circle, Grayton Beach 32459; (850) 534-5050; watercolorresort.com/florida-gulf-coast/restaurant.asp. Seafood is not just for dinner and lunch. It's also wonderful for breakfast, and Fish Out of Water at WaterColor Resort serves it daily until 11 a.m. They do serve lunch and dinner too, but I came for breakfast and ordered their shrimp-and-grits with a sunnyside-up egg. The food was as fine as the view, out across the sand dunes of Grayton Beach State Park and the turquoise Gulf of Mexico. If you arrive after 11 a.m., consider one of these entrees: miso-marinated bigeye tuna, Gulf black grouper with shrimp and mint chutney, or if you are ravenously hungry, you might opt for the substantial Seafood Grill with grouper, lobster, shrimp, and scallops in a chardonnay-saffron cream sauce.

Pensacola

Atlas Oyster House, 600 South Barracks Street, Pensacola, FL 32502;
(850) 470-0003; atlasoysterhouse.com. **The Fish House,** 600 South
Barracks Street, Pensacola 32502; (850) 470-0003; fishhousepensacola
.com. Atlas Oyster House and its sister restaurant the Fish House, next
door, are both part of the local Pensacola restaurant group Great Southern
Restaurants. Great Southern also operates Jackson's Steakhouse and
Palafox House, a special-events venue. In addition, they operate Great
Southern Cafe in Seaside (see the "Seaside" section). Pensacola native,
chef, and co-owner of Great Southern Restaurants Jim Shirley opened the
Fish House in 1998 and Atlas Oyster House in 2002.

From the diner's perspective, Atlas Oyster House and the Fish House
essentially function as one large restaurant. Both occupy a rambling
wooden structure that overlooks a cove off Pensacola Bay. Both offer outdoor seating to take in that scenic view. I picked Atlas and a table with a
view. Although both the Fish House and Atlas Oyster House are famous
for Jim Shirley's Shrimp and Grits à Ya Ya, shrimp and grito with spinach,

The City of Five Flags

Although St. Augustine, Florida, is considered the oldest continuously occupied city in America, Pensacolans are quick to point out that the founding of their city predates St. Augustine by 6 years. Spanish explorer Don Tristan de Luna built a settlement at this location in 1559, which he called Polonza, but 2 years later it was abandoned after a violent storm sank his fleet. More than a century would pass before Spain would return and build a permanent settlement here. Pensacola was also Florida's first capital, of the territory of West Florida, following the United States' purchase of Louisiana from France in 1803.

Pensacola is often called the City of Five Flags, as it was alternately occupied by the Spanish, the French, and the British before becoming part of the United States in 1821. And during the Civil War, both the Union and Confederate Armies were entrenched here, but the flag of the Confederacy flew over the city from 1861 to 1862.

Today Pensacola is a thriving midsize city best known for its Naval Air Station, where the Blue Angels are headquartered, and for its glistening white beaches just across the bridge on Pensacola Beach. Downtown Pensacola and the adjacent Seville Historic District have become lively gathering spots, with interesting shops, good restaurants, and regular concerts and festival events. With its close proximity to Alabama, Mississippi, and Louisiana, it is no surprise that Deep South and New Orleans Creole and Cajun cooking styles and preparation have had a significant influence on the food you will find in Pensacola and throughout the Panhandle.

applewood-smoked bacon, and Gouda cheese grits, I was intrigued by their Central American–style banana-leaf grouper, consisting of grilled black grouper that's wrapped in a banana leaf with ham and pineapple. The banana leaf does its job of keeping the grouper very moist and tender, and mine was delicious. And my side cup of gumbo was rich and spicy, with plenty of shrimp swimming around with the okra.

Their popular Sunday brunch also features some savory seafood items like a Cajun crawfish frittata, the aforementioned Shrimp and Grits à Ya Ya, and, naturally, oysters 5 different ways: on the half shell, blackened grilled, Rockefeller, Imperial, and Acadia (Cajun-style with crawfish, blue crab, and andouille sausage). Of late, Atlas Oyster House has also become one of Pensacola's hottest live music venues, hosting some of this area's top talent on Friday and Saturday nights.

H2O Cajun-Asian Grill, 12 Via De Luna Drive, Pensacola Beach 32561; (850) 916-2999; hiltonpensacolabeach.com/restaurants. Pensacola Beach's powdered-sugar sand and emerald-green Gulf waters have attracted tourists for ages, and hotels to accommodate them are plentiful. One popular hotel, the Hilton, also has a popular restaurant and sushi bar, H2O, which overlooks the hotel pool and the beach beyond it. I came for the much lauded sushi, but they didn't serve it at lunch, so I opted for their lobster Cobb salad, which came in a meal-size bowl with large hunks of fresh lobster, avocado, bacon, and crumbled blue cheese. H2O bills itself as Cajun/Asian fusion and indeed they do serve shrimp dumplings with sweet Thai chili sauce alongside fried alligator bites. Their Bonsai Sushi Bar begins serving at 5 p.m.

Joe Patti's Seafood Market, 524 South B Street, Pensacola 32502; (850) 432-3315; (800) 500-9929; joepattis.com. **Captain Joey Patti's Seafood Restaurant,** 610 South C Street, Pensacola 32502; (850) 434-3193; captainjoeysdeli.com. Sicilian-born Giuseppe "Joe" Patti came to the United States in 1919, eventually settling in Pensacola, where he found work as a deck hand on a commercial fishing boat. Within 5 years he was captaining his own boat. But when he met Anna, soon to be his wife, he decided to try shrimping in order to stay closer to home. Back then shrimp were sold more for bait than for food, and it was not an easy way to make a living. But this was the start of what would grow into one of the largest and most successful seafood markets in Florida, Joe Patti's Seafood. The sign out front says "Since 1931" but Joe Patti had actually been in business for himself since 1925. Today Joe Patti's Seafood Market takes up several city blocks at the end of "B" Street, with docks on Pensacola Bay on one side and Captain Joey Patti's Seafood Restaurant a block away on the other side on "C" Street. Through the decades Joe Patti's has supplied restaurants throughout northern Florida and shipped seafood to all fifty states. Now they have diversified into imported gourmet foods and wines, and the retail

seafood market has become their primary focus. It's almost overwhelming to walk into Joe Patti's, where mountains of fish, shrimp, oysters, crawfish, and lobsters greet you on the left, the market side. If it swims, it's here. A palpable energy permeates this place as customers line up, eager to pick out the best lobster, grouper, or shrimp to take home for dinner. Steer right and you'll walk into the gourmet wine market and deli, and eventually you will find their sushi counter.

Next door, Captain Joey Patti's Seafood Restaurant is their no-frills, just-good-fresh-seafood diner. I had their tasty crab roll sandwich on a hoagie roll. With two crab rolls, the sandwich was big enough that I had to eat it with a fork and knife. The family business diversification extends beyond food: The Patti family also owns Patti Marine Enterprises, a commercial shipbuilding company.

Joe Patti's is still family owned and operated. Joe and Anna's oldest son, Frank Patti, now in his mid-80s, is the boss, with other family members running the wine and gourmet shops and Frank's son Frank Jr. running the family's shipyard.

Perdido Key

Flora-Bama Lounge & Oyster Bar, 17401 Perdido Key Drive, Perdido Key 32507; (850) 492-0611; florabama.com. Ted and Ellen Tampary, along with their two sons Tony and Connie, had planned to debut the Flora-Bama Lounge in time for the start of summer in 1964. Perdido Key was a near-desolate barrier island back then. A bridge, from the Alabama side, had just been built in 1962. But their just-completed building burned down before they could open. Undeterred, they rebuilt and opened in October that year. It was, and still is, the quintessential beach roadhouse. What made the Flora-Bama unique was that it straddled the Florida-Alabama state line.

In 1978 the Tamparys sold to Joe Gilchrist and Pat McClellan, who knew a good thing when they saw it and changed nothing about the decor, but thought some live entertainment might lure more customers. They also came up with something that ultimately put the Flora-Bama on the national map: an annual (on the last full weekend in April) contest and beach party, the Interstate Mullet Toss. It is just what it sounds like: Who can throw a mullet the farthest, from one state to the next? The first time I

visited the Flora-Bama (back in the mid-1990s), it was still a 1-story build-ing. There was a state line painted down the middle of the bar's floor. I ordered my 2 dozen oysters on the half shell in one state and consumed them in the other. In 2004 Florida experienced a rash of state-crossing hurricanes. We got four in a 6-week period. Number 3, "Ivan," was one of those that hung out in the Atlantic and the Caribbean for a couple weeks before driving up into the Gulf of Mexico as a category 5. It had weakened to a category 3 by the time it made landfall, but it was still a monster, with a 50-mile-wide eye, and it landed right on the Florida-Alabama border. Some of the Flora-Bama withstood the onslaught, but a massive storm surge gut-ted it beyond repair. Ivan stands as one of the most devastating hurricanes ever to strike the Alabama/western Florida coast, so everyone assumed that this was the end of the Flora-Bama. But just like 40 years prior, eventu-ally it reopened.

In 2011 Gilchrist and McClellan added a third partner, John McKin-nis. In 2012 the Flora-Bama underwent a major renovation, and it's now 3 stories tall. They even salvaged much of the original bar and installed it on the third floor. To make the multiple bar rooms function more efficiently, they built a special "liquor room" with an automated system that pumps booze from hundreds of bottles, on demand, directly to the bars. Today the once lonely roadhouse is one of the most popular stops on this coast, booking name musicians like Kenny Chesney and Jimmy Buffet. They also serve up fresh-out-of-the-Gulf seafood including raw, Cajun-spicy, or "McClellan" (with bacon, onions, and Gouda cheese) oysters, and peel-and-eat or coconut-fried sweet jumbo royal red shrimp.

Over the years the Flora-Bama has found its way into the written word and song. It makes an appearance in John Grisham's 1992 thriller *The Pelican Brief* as well as Ace Atkins's 2015 Quinn Colson novel *The Redeem-ers*. And Jimmy Buffet's "Bama Breeze," Kenny Chesney's "Flora-Bama" and "Coastal," and Blake Shelton's "Good Ole Boys" all pay homage to the Flora-Bama.

Perry

Deal's Famous Oyster House, 2571 US Highway 98, Perry 32348; (850) 838-3325. A couple miles west of Perry on Highway 98, there is a low, concrete-block building off the side of the road that you could look right at and miss as you drive by. But don't judge a book by its cover . . . and don't judge an oyster joint by its exterior. Rachel Deal, with help from her husband, Ray, owned and ran Deal's Famous Oyster House for 40-some-odd years before retiring and selling the place to loyal longtime employee Zodie Horton in 2009. And Zodie knew not to change anything. The menu is truly South-meets-the-coast, with items like smoked mullet, soft-shell crab, fried dill pickles, and fried green beans as appetizers, and of course oysters, raw or fried. I had a basket of a dozen and a half fried oysters with grits, coleslaw, and these wonderful little curlicue-shape hush puppies, some of the sweetest hush puppies I've ever eaten. And they give you guava jelly to dip them in. Zodie has some musical talent as well and is not shy about performing at the height of lunch hour. She plays a pogo-stick contraption with built-in cymbals and a tambourine that one of her regular customers has labeled the Zodiephone.

Santa Rosa Beach

Old Florida Fish House, 5235 East County Road 30A, Santa Rosa Beach 32459; (850) 534-3045; oldfloridafishhouse.com. County Road 30A takes a brief turn inland just east of Seagrove and crosses brackish Eastern Lake. Here you'll find Old Florida Fish House, a rambling wooden restaurant on the lakeshore. They opened in 2005, but there are some interesting 100-year-old Florida touches. For instance, the bar and the tables are all made from century-old cypress lumber recovered from the bottom of Florida Panhandle rivers. Lumber harvesting and milling were dominant industries in northern Florida in the late 1800s and early 1900s. And cypress was one of the most sought-after types of wood. Lumberjacks tied logs together into massive rafts to transport them down rivers, but some of the logs didn't make the entire journey and sank to the bottom. Now some of that "sinker" river-reclaimed cypress is being recovered and used for home and furniture construction.

Old Florida Fish House has some old-Florida seafood items on its menu as well, like fried soft shell crab, pan roasted crab cakes, and a rich and spicy seafood gumbo. Additional menu items include sautéed grouper with butter-poached lump crab and shrimp, and an assortment of Old Florida Fried Platters that include shrimp, oysters, or grouper or mix and match.

Seagrove

Cafe Thirty-A, 3899 East County Road 30A, Seagrove 32459; (850) 231-2166; cafethirtya.com. After running Kat and Harri's Restaurant in Montgomery, Alabama, for 13 years, Harriet Crommelin opened Cafe Thirty-A in Seagrove, just in time for the arrival of Hurricane Opal. It was a nervous beginning to what has now become a 30A icon. With appetizers like Prince Edward Island mussels sautéed in coconut cream, white wine, and curry, and entrees like seafood cioppino, fresh-caught fish, clams, shrimp, and mussels with sausage, all in a tomato-garlic broth, Cafe Thirty-A qualifies as upscale dining. I opted for their pan-seared rare sesame-crusted yellowfin tuna, and it was outstanding. The food is gourmet and the atmosphere is elegant, but in 30A beach tradition, you can come as casual as you like.

Seaside

Bud & Alley's, 2236 East County Road 30A, Seaside 32459; (850) 231-5900; budandalleys.com. Right next to the Shrimp Shack is Seaside's first (and by my personal estimation, one of Florida's best) restaurants, Bud & Alley's. Back in 1987 Seaside had yet to be "discovered." Robert Davis and his wife, Daryl, had been building their Florida Cracker–style beach houses on the 80-acre piece of land inherited from his grandfather for only 6 years when surfing buddies Dave Rauschkolb and Scott Witcoski approached Davis about putting a restaurant on the beach side of County Road 30A. They decided to name it after Robert and Daryl's dachshund Bud and Scott's cat Alley. In 2006 Scott sold his interest back to Dave, but Alley's silhouette still joins Bud's on the sign. While not exclusively a seafood restaurant, two-thirds of Bud & Alley's menu is comprised of seafood. Their crab cakes are spectacular and probably the most popular dish, but I'm

The Birth of Seaside

In 1978 developer Robert Davis inherited 80 acres of undeveloped land nestled between Grayton Beach State Park and Seagrove that had belonged to his grandfather. In 1981 he began building Seaside. Davis envisioned a small beach town with sand-and-shell walkways winding between pastel-shaded wood-frame bungalows, a reminder of his childhood summers spent on the beach at Seagrove. At that time he didn't know it would evolve into the model for New Urbanism, a now much-heralded community design concept that seeks to promote a small-town atmosphere: homes with front porches that encourage interaction with your neighbors, and pedestrian-and bicycle-friendly pathways, all within walking distance of the town's commercial center. It's an old idea reborn as something new.

The popular 1998 movie The Truman Show (starring Jim Carrey) brought some national attention to Seaside. Production designers needed the perfect idyllic small town as a backdrop. They considered building a movie-set town from scratch on Paramount's lot until someone showed them a picture of Seaside.

partial to their seared diver scallops over grits with roasted peppers and bacon.

Great Southern Cafe, 83 Central Square, Seaside 32459; (850) 231-7327; thegreatsoutherncafe.com. Great Southern Cafe does a praiseworthy job of representing what I call Panhandle cuisine. It blends coastal Florida seafood with good-old southern Georgia and Alabama and spicy New Orleans cooking styles. What you get are dishes like crab cakes and fried green tomatoes with roasted red pepper rémoulade, and Shrimp and Grits à Ya Ya: shrimp-and-grits with spinach, applewood-smoked bacon, and Gouda cheese grits. Yep. The same Shrimp and Grits à Ya Ya as the Fish House and Atlas Oyster House in Pensacola prepare, all part of the same Great Southern Restaurants Group, based in Pensacola. Great Southern

Cafe's menu is about half seafood, but the seafood that they offer definitely hits the spot. Try their Seafood Celebration, a platter with grilled fresh-catch fish, blackened shrimp, fried oysters, and the best part: smoked-corn tartar sauce.

The Shrimp Shack, 2236 East County Road 30A, Seaside 32459; (850) 231-3799; sweetwilliamsltd.com/shrimp_shack.asp. The tiny walk-up Shrimp Shack, in sublime Seaside, sits just behind a sand dune on the beach side of scenic County Road 30A. I always order a basket of steamed, peppered peel-and-eat Gulf pink shrimp (or royal reds) and a tall fresh-squeezed lemonade, then kick back on their beach-sand-on-the-floor screened porch, and feast while watching beachgoers come and go. They

also have oysters and buttered Florida lobster tail with steamed corn on the cob on the side. Somehow it all tastes just a little bit better when you're close enough to the Gulf to smell the salt in the air and feel the sea breeze.

St. Marks

Riverside Cafe, 69 Riverside Drive, St. Marks 32355; (850) 925-5668; riversidebay.com. Posey's Oyster Bar in St. Marks, a Florida Panhandle icon since 1929, belongs in the Florida Oyster Bar Hall of Fame. Sadly, in

Gruntin' Worms

When I was growing up in Florida in the 1960s, every kid with a Zebco rod and reel or a cane pole knew that to catch fish, you had to have worms. I spent many a summer day at my good friends the Hills' lake house, where we would fish for bream. If we were lucky, we might hook a bass. Earthworms, or night crawlers (*Eisenia hortensis* for those of you who insist on knowing the Latin name), bought at the corner store have long been the bait of choice, because fish love them. But no one seems to be certain why. Earthworms are not aquatic. They live in soil, so they are not a natural food for fish. Speculation leans toward it having something to do with all the wiggling, which attracts a fish's attention, or maybe earthworms are particularly pleasantly pungent to fish.

There's a tiny town about 45 miles south-southwest of Tallahassee that has been annually celebrating the slimy wrigglers since 2000. Sopchoppy (population 457 as of the 2010 census) sits nestled in a bend in the Ochlockonee River. The name is likely a mispronunciation of two Creek Indian words that describe the river: *sokhe* and *chapke*, meaning "twisted" and "long." Or the Creek Indians might have been describing something else: worms. Worms have put Sopchoppy on the map. The variety that breeds in this area's soil is particularly fat and long, a fisherman's dream. The method used to bring them to the surface is called "gruntin'." The worm grunter's tools are a wooden stake and a flattened iron paddle. Something amazing happens when a grunter drives the stake into the ground and grinds the iron paddle against it: Worms come wriggling out of the ground by the hundreds. The grunting noise that the grinding makes sends a vibration through the ground that makes the little slimy guys crazy.

On the second weekend in April, Sopchoppy holds its annual Worm Gruntin' Festival and Worm Grunters' Ball. There's lots of good food and live entertainment, and they choose a Worm Queen. The highlight, however, is the Worm Gruntin' Contest, a competition to see who can grunt up the most worms in 15 minutes. In 1972 Charles Kuralt brought worm gruntin' to the attention of the outside world, much to the chagrin of locals. Following that publicity, the US Forest Service began requiring a permit and charging fees for gruntin'.

2005 Hurricane Dennis flooded St. Marks and closed Posey's forever. But all is not lost. Next door to Posey's original location, you will find Stan and Karen West's Riverside Cafe serving fresh-shucked oysters and seafood baskets, and hosting some lively local entertainment. Stan, along with his original Riverside Cafe partner Dave Vaillancourt, also started the St. Marks Stone Crab Festival, which has now grown into a community-wide event.

St. Marks: A Tiny Place with a Long, Rich History

The tiny riverside village of St. Marks sits at the confluence of the Wakulla and St. Marks Rivers, 20 miles due south of Tallahassee and 3 miles upstream from the Gulf of Mexico. Spanish missionaries built the Mission San Marcos de Apalache here in the early 1600s. In 1680 Spanish troops built Fort San Marcos de Apalache, which through the next 200 years was alternately rebuilt and occupied by Spanish, French, British, and eventually American troops. Some remains of the fort can still be seen at its site just off SR 363.

By the early 1800s St. Marks had become an important shipping port. The Tallahassee Railroad Company built one of the state's first railroads, from Tallahassee to St. Marks, in 1837. Mules pulled the cars. Today that route has been converted into the Tallahassee–St. Marks Historic Trail, a Rails-to-Trails project.

Fishing, kayaking, bicycling on the St. Marks Historic Trail, and eating oysters are the main reasons people come to St. Marks today, but there is more to see. The St. Marks National Wildlife Refuge, just 4 miles east, is home to a wide variety of coastal woodlands wildlife, everything from anhingas to alligators. The 80-foot-tall St. Marks Lighthouse, at the south end of SR 59 in the wildlife refuge, was built in 1829.

Steinhatchee

Roy's Restaurant, 100 1st Avenue SW, Steinhatchee 32359; (352) 498-5000; roys-restaurant.com. Roy's Restaurant, overlooking the mouth of the Steinhatchee River, opened in 1969. Locals Ben and Linda Wicker have owned and operated it for years. Their menu includes many local-caught specialties like soft-shell crab, blue-crab claws, and crab-stuffed flounder. I couldn't decide on just one thing to try, so I ordered a grilled seafood platter with shrimp, oysters, flounder, an in-shell deviled crab, and a generous heap of that Steinhatchee specialty, bay scallops. This is good, simple, fresh seafood, and you can enjoy it while looking right out over the waters where much of it likely came from. Roy's also makes their own soups and chowders, like Oyster stew and New England–style clam chowder, but the best is their Kickin' Crab and Sweet Corn Chowder, with just enough hot sauce in it to make it kick.

Scalloping

The bite-size and sweet-tasting bay scallop could be consid
ered the candy of the seafood world. Scallop shells are easy to
spot. They have the distinctive two-finned shell that the Shell Oil
Company uses in their familiar logo. Generally speaking, scallops
come in two varieties: the smaller "bay" scallops and the larger,
deepwater (sometimes called "diver") scallops. Bay scallops can
be collected both recreationally and commercially, while deepwater scallops are almost exclusively the domain of commercial
harvesters. "Diver" originally referred to how deepwater scallops
were collected—by scuba diving—although these days it usually
just refers to any larger deepwater varieties, which are usually
collected with nets.

Recreational bay scalloping has always been a favorite
Florida pastime. Florida scallopers must have a Florida Saltwater
Fishing License and can only collect within the boundaries of the
Bay Scallop Harvest Zone, along the Gulf Coast "Big Bend" area
from Mexico Beach (just west of Apalachicola) down to Aripeka
(just north of Tarpon Springs). Scallop season runs from the last
weekend in June through the last weekend in September. There is
a daily bag limit of 1 pint of shucked scallop meat (or 2 gallons of
whole still-in-the-shell scallops) per person. Bay scallops usually
reside in 5 to 10 feet of water, nestled in grassy-bottom coastal
areas. To collect them, simply swim to the bottom and grab as
many scallops as you can on one breath. Mask, snorkel, fins, and a
mesh collection bag are all acceptable tools of the trade, but use
of scuba gear is strictly prohibited for collecting bay scallops.

History along the Steinhatchee River

The village of Steinhatchee, at the mouth of the Steinhatchee River, is a popular launching point for fishing in the Gulf, but scalloping on the grass flats just out from the mouth of the river is Steinhatchee's prime attraction.

It is pronounced Steen-HAT-chee, by the way. It means "river of man," or some interpret it as "dead man's river" in the Creek language. In 1838, prior to his presidency, General Zachary Taylor ordered the construction of Fort Frank Brooke on the banks of the Steinhatchee River during the height of the Second Seminole War, but it was abandoned 2 years later. Today scuba divers still find artifacts like buttons from military jackets, tools, and utensils on the bottom of the river. The small settlement that subsequently grew here was called Stephensville until 1931 when the name was changed to match the river.

Tallahassee

Kool Beanz Cafe, 921 Thomasville Road, Tallahassee 32303; (850) 224-2466; kool-beanz.com. I know it sounds like a coffee shop but it's not. What it is is an innovative, fun-atmosphere cafe that takes "fusion" seriously. While not exclusively a seafood restaurant, fish and shellfish do feature prominently on the Kool Beanz menu. They print a new one every day, based on what they are able to get fresh that morning, and on what the chef's creative inclination is in the kitchen that day. For example, the day I was there, they offered (among many other items) pecan-floured cobia with jalapeño tartar sauce, and a tortilla-crusted grouper with guajillo (a type of chili) sauce. I had jerked sea scallops with pineapple-chili salsa, coconut black-bean sauce, and maduros (ripe, fried plantains) over cilantro rice that was outstanding. Kool Beanz is famous for their imagination in the kitchen, with regular dishes like British pub staple fish-and-chips made with beer-battered tilefish, and tortilla-crusted amberjack with salsa verde and a corn-lime crema sauce. It's no surprise that some of this area's best chefs have worked in Kool Beanz's kitchen, including Florida's Official Culinary Ambassador, Justin Timineri. (See "A Conversation with Florida's Official Culinary Ambassador, Chef Justin Timineri" on p. 42.)

The Seineyard Restaurant, 8056 Woodville Highway, Tallahassee 32305; (850) 421-9191; theseineyard.com. **The Other Seineyard Restaurant,** 1660-6 North Monroe Street, Tallahassee 32303; (850) 480-9191, theotherseineyard.com. There are two Seineyard Restaurant locations. Sam and Starr Dunlap opened the original in 1995 in Woodville,

A Conversation with Florida's Official Culinary Ambassador, Chef Justin Timineri

Justin Timineri
Executive Chef
Dept. of Agriculture

"I knew from a very young age that I wanted to be a chef, really the only thing I ever wanted to be," Justin Timineri explained to me when I visited him at his Florida Department of Agriculture office in Tallahassee. Chef Timineri is the Culinary Ambassador and State Chef for the Florida Department of Agriculture and Consumer Services. His recipes and advice, along with a compendium of information about Florida-specific food, can be found on the department's website FreshFromFlorida .com. "My families, on both sides, were all phenomenal cooks, so there was always something going on in the kitchen."

Justin, who grew up in Tallahassee, started working in restaurants at an early age. He didn't go to culinary school, instead earning his culinary credentials through work experience at Tallahassee restaurants Mosaic and Kool Beanz Cafe, and working with Chef Albert Ughetto (founder of Albert's Provence in Tallahassee and former executive chef on Jacques Cousteau's *Calypso*). Justin has been an event chef at NASCAR races, PGA tournaments, and the Kentucky Derby. As assistant chef at the Governor's Mansion, he has worked for Governors Jeb Bush, Charlie Crist, and Rick Scott. In 2006 he was chosen out of 60 entrants to become the Florida Department of Agriculture's Culinary Ambassador for the State of Florida.

Naturally, seafood features prominently on FreshFrom Florida.com, and I asked Justin about some of his favorites. "Florida clams are great, often overlooked, and relatively inexpensive. We also have amazing shrimp, not just the pinks and whites but also royal reds, the more rare deepwater shrimp, as well as rock shrimp, another of my favorites. My very favorite fish is probably pompano."

A big part of Justin's job is educating consumers. "It's important for consumers to understand not just what's fresh but what the harvest seasons for various types of fish are, and also where they are harvested." On buying seafood he explained, "Consider buying the fish whole. That way you can make sure you're getting the freshest possible product. You can look at the gills to see that they are pink. You can look at the eyes to see that they are clear (not milky). And you can smell it to make sure it has a nice sea breezy and a little-bit-salty scent."

On cooking that seafood Justin says, "My advice to home cooks is to start with some of the less expensive seafood, like shrimp or clams, then work up to fin fish, like mahi. It'll take some practice. A common seafood-cooking mistake is overcooking. So I remind people that when you pull something out of the pan or the oven, there is carry-over cooking. It's still hot and continues to cook. Done in the pan can be *over*done on the plate."

He tells me that he is seeing a positive shift in consumers' approach to food preparation. "Certainly we have become accustomed to going to the grocery store and buying anything we want any time of year. So I like to issue this challenge: Try, instead, letting the market dictate your meal. Go to your market and find what's fresh and in season. Buy those ingredients and then go find the recipe that has those ingredients. Both for fruits and vegetables, and for seafood, let what is fresh and in season dictate what you're going to cook. This is what FreshFromFlorida .com is all about: getting consumers to understand the growing seasons, when things are in peak, so they can purchase it fresh and make a wonderful meal from their Florida food."

a community just south of Tallahassee. Their Other Seineyard Restaurant, opened in 2011, is tucked away in the corner of a Tallahassee shopping plaza. If you're looking for a simple, inexpensive, and casual seafood-platter kind of place, this is it. I went to the Other Seineyard Restaurant and had a grilled catfish-fingers sandwich with cheese grits, all quite tasty. The catfish was very fresh, and it comes from local farms.

Seine Netting

"Seineyard" refers to a beach where seine nets would be pulled just offshore to catch mullet, a practice that was common 50 years ago. I used to pull seine nets with my Uncle Manuel Corral and cousins Chris and Kent at Indian Rocks Beach and Belleair Beach back in the 1960s and '70s. As the youngest, my job was to swim out beyond the net to scare schools of mullet (or whatever might be swimming by) in toward the nets. My uncle and cousins would pull the net out from the shore and then back around in a big arc and back to the beach. Nothing was more exciting than anticipating the catch as they muscled the net back onto shore. You knew when the catch was big because the net was harder to pull, and fish would jump over the top to escape. We always caught mullet, but also sheepshead, whiting, and sometimes stingrays, mackerel, or sea trout. Back then the nets were 50 feet long, and no fishing license was required.

Today the practice of beach seine netting falls under Florida State fishing regulations, just like saltwater rod-and-reel fishing: Each person working the net must have a fishing license. The size and design of the net is restricted—it can be no longer than 20 feet and no larger than 500 square feet. The net's hole openings can be no more than 2 inches wide, and it cannot be made from monofilament (twine is preferred). And of course, all state fishing season and bag limits apply. Some beaches have local ordinances that prohibit beach seine netting, so inquire beforehand if you think you might want to give it a try.

Shell Oyster Bar, 114 Oakland Avenue, Tallahassee 32301; (850) 224-9919; facebook.com/ShellOysterBar. Shell Oyster Bar sits just 5 blocks from the state capitol (but literally on the "other side of the railroad tracks"). It's been here since 1945 and shares a piece of property with Maner's Drain and Change Garage (which looks like it's been closed for years, but who can tell?). It doesn't look much like a restaurant from the outside, but inside it's packed every day at lunch. The clientele is an eclectic mix. You will likely see an auto mechanic sitting next to a state senator. The menu—raw oysters, fried seafood baskets, and the like—may not be out of the ordinary, but the social dynamic is priceless.

Northeast

Florida's northeast coast bills itself as the "First Coast," and for good reason. Although Christopher Columbus is routinely credited with "discovering" America, he never got any farther than the Bahamas and the Caribbean. Columbus never actually set foot on mainland America. It was another European explorer (who had sailed with Columbus on earlier expeditions), Spaniard Juan Ponce de Leon, who first landed on Florida's beaches on April 2, 1513. There is some argument about the exact location where de Leon landed. Depending on which historian you talk to, it was either a bit north of where St. Augustine is now or just south of Daytona at Ponce Inlet, or just south of Cape Canaveral near Melbourne.

Ponce de Leon was ostensibly searching for gold and Oriental pearls, but he was also obsessed with finding something else: a special spring rumored to produce water with youth-giving properties. This "Fountain of Youth" was actually supposed to have been on the island of Bimini in the Bahamas (Bimini was the old name for Andros, not the Bimini we know today). After doing some exploring he figured out that he had found a place too big to be an island, and promptly claimed possession of the new land in the name of King Ferdinand of Spain. It was Easter time and the flowers and trees that he found there reminded him of Spain's "Pasque Florida," the Feast of Flowers, so he named it Florida.

◆•• ———————— ◆•◆• ——————— ••◆

Brett's Waterway Cafe, 1 South Front Street, Fernandina Beach
32034; (904) 261-2660; facebook.com/brettswaterwaycafe. Brett's, which
opened in 1983, is the only downtown Fernandina restaurant actually on
the waterfront. It sits out on the docks, overlooking both shrimping boats
and pleasure yachts. You'll find good Southern-influenced dishes here like
shrimp-and-grits and fried green tomatoes. I had barbecue-grilled shrimp
over cheese grits with collard greens, while enjoying the view of the St.
Marys River.

The Crab Trap, 31 North 2nd Street, Fernandina Beach 32034; (904)-
261-4749; ameliacrabtrap.com. I see crabmeat as the seafood equivalent
to the food of the gods, but there must be a hundred seafood joints in
Florida named "The Crab Trap," some of them mediocre, so I was skeptical
when I walked into this one in Fernandina Beach. But it turns out these
people really know their crabs. I had the steamed Dungeness crab, legs
and body. If you have ever eaten one of those wonderful sidewalk-cart

crab cocktails at Fisherman's Wharf in San Francisco, then you've had Dungeness crab. It's a Pacific Coast crab. I rate it high on the "amount of cracking-work-to-meat-acquired ratio" scale. Stone crab claws are at the top of that list, but Dungeness crab comes in second. The claw shells are soft enough that you can crack them with your hands. You don't need the cracker. There's lots of meat in the body too. It's messy, but it's worth it. Yes, the Dungeness crab is a Pacific crab, but the Crab Trap's was very fresh, so they must have flown it here in a Lockheed SR-71. If messy is not your thing, they also offer a full assortment of oyster, shrimp, and fresh-catch platters, seafood casserole, and shrimp Creole. Also noteworthy are their fluffy hush puppies.

It's always more interesting to dine in a historic building, and there are plenty in Fernandina. The Crab Trap is in the Sydel Building, named for the two brothers who built it in 1877. It was one of the first brick buildings

From Boomtown to Historic Destination

Fernandina Beach, on the north end of Amelia Island, began to boom in the mid-1800s. Luxury steamers from the Northeast brought wealthy vacationers to the port town at the mouth of the St. Marys River, and soon elegant inns and palatial Victorian mansions began to spring up in the blocks north and south of the town's main street, Centre Street. Fernandina also became a vital shipping port. Then the 1898 Spanish-American War generated even more shipping and rail business. But just after the turn of the century, railroad magnate Henry Flagler decided to bypass Fernandina and divert his rail passengers to St. Augustine, where Flagler had opened his Ponce de Leon Hotel. Fernandina's boom fizzled, but it managed to survive the subsequent decades. In 1973 downtown Fernandina Beach received designation as a National Register of Historic Places Historic District, and that was expanded in 1987 to what today encompasses about 50 blocks. In 1977 Fernandina began renovating Centre Street. Today Fernandina is a thriving and picturesque small town that has embraced its history. Quaint shops, boutique inns, bed-and-breakfasts, and superb restaurants abound.

constructed in Fernandina after an 1876 fire swept through the town. It contained a general store, then later the offices of the local newspaper, the *Nassau County Leader*. Owner Richard Germano opened the Crab Trap here in 1979 and still runs it today, along with his daughter Holly.

España Restaurant, 22 South 4th Street, Fernandina Beach 32034; (904) 261-7700; espanadowntown.com. Chef Roberto Pestana and his wife, Marina, came to Fernandina and opened España in 2004. Roberto had been operating the Pompano Beach restaurant that his Portuguese-

born parents had opened 2 decades prior. España is very much a traditional Portuguese-style (and Spanish) restaurant. Their extensive tapas menu features many seafood offerings, like *gambas al ajillo* (shrimp in garlic sauce), *almejas borrachas* (drunken clams) with onions and garlic in white wine sauce, and of course ceviche. Their authentic Portuguese and Spanish seafood entrees include, among others, Pargo Olé, spicy snapper with shrimp and roasted poblano; and *mero a Lisboeta* (Grouper Lisbon), topped with tomato, onion, capers, and olives, the dish that I feasted on the last time I was here. Their specialties, however, are *paella marinera* (seafood paella) with clams, shrimp, lobster, scallops, mussels, and calamari, plus whatever the fresh fish of the day is, and *Calderada de mariscos* (Portuguese fisherman's stew). Both are prepared to order and are only for 4 or more people.

Joe's 2nd Street Bistro, 14 South 2nd Street, Fernandina Beach 32034; (904) 321-2558; joesbistro.com. Chef Ricky Pigg (previously an executive chef with the Stoney River Legendary Steaks chain) and his wife,

Mari, bought Joe's 2nd Street Bistro in 2012. Joe's occupies a quaint 1903 Charleston single–style house with a courtyard alongside and a picket fence out front. If it's possible to pull off casual and elegant all at the same time, Joe's does it. I started my meal with their refreshing tuna martini: seared and cubed ahi tuna tossed with avocado, mango, pineapple, and cilantro. Then for my entree I had their spectacular seafood bouillabaisse, a huge bowl filled with lobster claw meat, plump shrimp, deepwater scallops, littleneck clams, and fish, all stewed in a rich saffron-and-tomato broth. At lunch they serve shrimp po'boys, crab and eggs with applewood bacon and lump crab, shrimp-and-grits, and shrimp-and-lobster mac and cheese. Additional dinner seafood entrees include farfalle (bowtie) pasta with pan-seared salmon, linguine with shrimp and scallops, and grouper fillet grilled in a corn husk wrapper.

Lulu's, 11 South 7th Street, Fernandina Beach 32034; (904) 432-8394; lulusamelia.com. You will find Lulu's in a small carriage house next to one of Fernandina's historic Victorian homes, the Thompson House, a block north of Fernandina's main street, Centre Street. British-born Brian Grimley and his wife, Melanie, bought the restaurant in 2010 (it had originally opened in 2000) and made it their own. Brian's dishes tend toward Charleston-style low country and New Orleans Cajun, but the menu alters daily depending on what they can get fresh locally, so naturally this area's specialty shrimp features regularly. I had their mouthwatering grilled shrimp tacos with fresh-chopped salsa on fresh-baked corn tortillas, all

Shrimp is King

At the risk of sounding ironic, when it comes to seafood, shrimp is king in Fernandina. The modern commercial shrimping techniques used today had their beginnings here. Traditionally shrimp had been caught using two boats and a seine net. But in 1913 Billy Corkum, a Gloucester, Massachusetts, fisherman, came to Fernandina and adapted an otter trawl net—essentially a large bag-shaped net towed behind a single boat—to shrimping. It dramatically improved efficiency and it's the method almost all commercial shrimpers still use today.

drizzled with a savory cream sauce. Here are some more equally enticing entrees: shrimp Alfredo with chorizo and pancetta, andouille-crusted grouper, Parmesan-crusted flounder with sweet pea and corn gnocchi, and alligator sausage and scallops with roasted pepper *agrodolce* (an Italian sweet-and-sour sauce) on fried polenta. They also do a Sunday brunch where they serve crab cake Benedict and fried oyster Benedict.

Timoti's Seafood Shak, 21 North 3rd Street, Fernandina Beach 32034; (904) 310-6550; timotis.com. Local restaurateur and former city commissioner Tim Poynter (who also owns Cafe Karibo and Karibrew) opened Timoti's in 2012 and put local chef Brian McCarthy in charge of the kitchen. "Local" seems to be Timoti's theme. They get their seafood fresh from Fernandina's docks every morning. Don't let the reasonable prices and walk-up counter fool you: This is outstanding seafood. I had their tasty tuna poke with coconut rice, avocado, kelp, and sesame seeds, with a sweet teriyaki sauce. Then I came back the next day for their luscious lobster

roll. Actually, they give you two hand-size lobster rolls, which makes them easier to pick up and eat. You can also feast on their shrimp, oyster, clam, or fresh catch baskets, which are fried, grilled, or blackened. They also have shrimp or oyster po'boys, crab burgers, shrimp burgers, and blackened mahi sandwiches.

Jacksonville

Blue Fish Restaurant & Oyster Bar, 3551 St. Johns Avenue, Jacksonville 32205; (904) 387-0700; bluefishjax.com. Blue Fish Restaurant sits among boutiques and cafes in Jacksonville's tony Avondale neighborhood, in the Riverside Historic District. Their Elevated Avondale upstairs bar is a popular entertainment spot, but their seafood is also a big draw. I started with a very spicy barbecued shrimp in garlic, rosemary, and Worcestershire sauce. It came with slices of crusty French bread for dipping. For a main course I tried one of the specials: Indian style pan-seared wahoo with a sweet apple, tomato, and chipotle chutney piled on top, which was very tasty. A couple other regular dinner entrées that sound appetizing are the seared scallops and shrimp over mac and cheese and the

The St. Johns River

The St. Johns River is Florida's longest at over 300 miles. It's also one of only a handful of rivers in the United States that flows from south to north, where it spills out into the Atlantic Ocean at Jacksonville. French Huguenot Jean Ribault arrived near the mouth of the St. Johns River in 1562 and noted the strategic importance of the location, but instead of building a settlement here, he continued north up to South Carolina. Two years after Ribault passed through, another Frenchman, René Goulaine de Laudonnière, established Fort Caroline on the banks of the St. Johns, but this didn't set well with the Spanish, since Juan Ponce de Leon had claimed all of Florida for Spain almost 50 years before. So in 1565 Spain sent Pedro Menendez de Avile to run the French out of Florida, reclaiming the fort and surrounding settlement for Spain. Spain would go on to control this area until 1821 when it became part of the United States. For a while during the Civil War, there was a Confederate fort here on the south banks of the St. Johns, in what is now the village of Mayport, but the first permanent base, the Mayport Naval Station, did not go up until 1942. Today it is home to the United States' third-largest Navy surface fleet.

black-and-white sesame tuna seared rare with a soy ginger glaze. Enticing lunch items include horseradish-crusted catch of the day, shrimp-and-grits, and jambalaya.

Clark's Fish Camp, 12903 Hood Landing Road, Jacksonville 32258; (904) 268-3474; clarksfishcamp.com. In a similar vein to the Yearling in Cross Creek and the Linger Lodge in Bradenton, Clark's Fish Camp specializes in Florida Cracker cuisine, with adventurous menu items like smoked eel, gator ribs, frog legs, and fried snake (they don't specify what type of snake). A more conventional diner has choices too: steamed peel-and-eat shrimp; steamed clams; oysters, raw or Rockefeller; and crab cakes. The rustic restaurant hangs out over Julington Creek (farther upstream

from the Julington Creek Fish Camp) and, like the Linger Lodge, features lots of exotic taxidermy.

Julington Creek Fish Camp, 12760 San Jose Boulevard, Jacksonville 32223; (904) 886-2267; julingtoncreekfishcamp.com. Additional locations: **North Beach Fish Camp,** 100 1st Street, Neptune Beach 32266; (904) 249-3474. **Palm Valley Fish Camp,** 299 Roscoe Boulevard North, Ponte Vedra Beach 32082; (904) 285-3200. Julington Creek Fish Camp is one of 3 "Fish Camp" seafood restaurants operated by local restaurateurs Ben and Liza Groshell, who got their start with Marker 32. This one overlooks Julington Creek, a tributary off the St. Johns River, on the south side of Jacksonville. Their menu gives a nod toward Southern style cooking with items like pimento cheese spread, fried green tomatoes, and shrimp-and-grits, but there's a lot more, like seafood linguine in garlic-tomato sauce, and iron-skillet-fried brook trout with arugula and bacon. I was here for lunch and wanted something lighter, so I ordered toasted

sesame–seared yellowfin tuna, which came over a generous arugula salad, with a tangy-sweet teriyaki dressing. Their dinner menu is a seafood smorgasbord, with grilled salmon doused in horseradish hollandaise, roast cod fillet with brown butter, garlic, and lemon, iron-skillet-fried brook trout, and Low Country Boil for Two. The Groshells' two other "Fish Camp" restaurants are in Ponte Vedra and at Neptune Beach, both with similar menus.

Mayport

Safe Harbor Seafood Market and Restaurant, 4378 Ocean Street #3, Mayport 32233; (904) 246-4911; safeharborseafoodmayport.com. Although it is less than a mile across, there is no bridge that spans the mouth of the St. Johns River at Mayport. Instead, the Mayport Ferry has connected the north and south banks of the St. Johns River here since 1894. Between the ferry crossing, the naval station, and many shrimping boat fleets headquartering here, the tiny village of Mayport has plenty to keep it busy. Safe Harbor Seafood Market and Restaurant opened in Mayport as a wholesale seafood market in 1988, then in 2013 it expanded to include the retail market and restaurant. Their long row of iced cases is filled with every type of fish and shellfish imaginable, all just pulled out of the sea. The restaurant makes great use of that resource so you can dine on very fresh crab, lobster, grouper, tuna, oysters, and of course shrimp, which I felt obligated to order. Mine were marvelous steamed peel-and-eat jumbo Atlantic whites, seasoned with Old Bay.

St. Augustine

Aunt Kate's on the River, 612 Euclid Avenue, St. Augustine 32084; (904) 829-1105; aunt-kates.com. The "Kate" in Aunt Kate's refers to Catherine Usina, who with her husband, Frank, began serving seafood meals to winter visitors to St. Augustine back in 1900. Today Aunt Kate's on the River (a dozen blocks from the Atlantic Ocean on the Tolomato River) is doing the same, but the visitors come year-round. From a picnic table on their back porch, overlooking the river and Mike's Place Bait House, I had the Caribbean shrimp salad roll, creamy and spicy, on a toasted bun. They also have soft-shell crab and flounder sandwiches, Low Country Boil, shrimp-and-grits, fried oysters, lump crab cakes, scallops

What's in a Name? Changing the Names of Fish to Make Them More Marketable

If *slimehead* were a restaurant's special fresh catch of the day, would you order it? Yeah, me neither. But if it's *orange roughy*, you bet! Orange roughy, a type of deep-ocean perch, is delicious, with light, flaky, and flavorful meat, and a fish whose original name was "slimehead." St. Peters fish may not sound unappetizing, just uninteresting. But call it "tilapia" and suddenly it's on every restaurant's menu. The Patagonia toothfish is a large (sometimes up to 200 pounds) cold-water cod that fishermen would routinely throw back. But rename it "Chilean sea bass" (and it's not even a bass!) and it becomes a prized special of the day. Goosefish, a bottom dweller with a giant menacing-looking flat head, is now "monkfish," the tail meat of which is quite tasty. As for mahimahi, well, it's obvious why that name has supplanted "dolphin": Nobody wants to think they're eating Flipper.

This all started back in the early 1970s when the National Marine Fisheries Service (now part of NOAA, the National Oceanic and Atmospheric Administration, within the Department of Commerce) decided that fish with unappetizing names might be getting a bad rap. They ran surveys, hired a Chicago marketing consulting firm called Brand Group Incorporated, and at one point even hired the United States Army Food Research Laboratories in Natick, Massachusetts, all in an attempt to figure out how to rebrand unfortunately named fish. The program continued well into the 1980s, and ultimately quite a few fish names were changed. The bad part is that in some cases the name changes worked so well that some renamed fish, like the orange roughy and the Chilean sea bass, became overfished to the point of endangerment.

(fried, grilled, boiled, or blackened), and a specialty: Minorcan clam chowder.

Catch 27, 17 Hypolita Street, St. Augustine 32080; (904) 217-8190; catchtwentyseven.com. Catch 27 occupies one of the many old houses on a narrow cobblestone street in the heart of St. Augustine's historic district. A chalkboard at the entrance will tell you what they have fresh that day. I had a spicy-creamy version of shrimp-and-grits. They put blacken-spiced shrimp in a cream-sherry sauce and on a polenta cake, in lieu of traditional grits, and it worked well. They also have St. Augustine gumbo with clams, shrimp, sausage, and Minorcan spices; shrimp and fish tacos; and blue-crab cakes.

The Columbia Restaurant, 98 St. George Street, St. Augustine 32084; (904) 824-3341; columbiarestaurant.com. See main listing on p. 115.

O'Steen's Restaurant, 205 Anastasia Boulevard, St. Augustine 32080; (904) 829-6974; augustine.com/restaurant/osteens-restaurant. Railroad employee Robert "Chief" O'Steen and his wife, Jennie, opened their restaurant, across the bridge from old St. Augustine, in 1965 following a railroad strike. Longtime employee Lonnie Pomar, who started working there when he was just 12 years old, bought it from the O'Steens in 1983. The small restaurant, with 16 tables and a 6-person counter, and its menu have essentially not changed since it opened. O'Steen's does not take reservations or credit cards. Walk up to an outside window and put your name on the list and they'll call you. This is a locals' place. When I was here, I noticed lots of conversation between tables. Everybody knew everybody else. O'Steen's is known for good, fresh, simple food, in generous portions. They are most famous for their shrimp, fried in a cracker meal batter spiced with locally grown datil peppers, a St. Augustine Minorcan (Minorcans arrived here in the late 1700s) specialty. But instead of shrimp, I had their fresh catch of the day—broiled flounder—with hush puppies, green beans, and rice and gravy, and it definitely hit the spot.

The Reef Restaurant, 4100 Coastal Highway, St. Augustine 32084; (904) 824-8008; thereefstaugustine.com. The Reef Restaurant sits atop a beach bluff a few miles north of St. Augustine. Diners have a commanding view overlooking the Atlantic Ocean. It originally opened in 1989 as Compton's Restaurant. The Reef's menu features an extensive

The Oldest City in Florida

St. Augustine is not just the oldest city in Florida, it's the oldest continuously occupied city in the United States and one of Florida's most popular destinations. Narrow avenues and alleyways interweave its historic district, and horse-drawn carriages clip-clop along the roads. Some of the older structures are over 250 years old, built during St. Augustine's British occupation from 1763 to 1784. Vacationers and history buffs come to see the historic district and adjacent Fort Castillo de San Marcos, constructed by the Spanish beginning in 1672. Nearby beaches are also a draw, and quaint inns, bed-and-breakfasts, and good restaurants are plentiful.

list of seafood items, some of them a bit exotic, like zarzuela bouillabaisse (a version originating from the Catalonia region of Spain), Scottish gravlax salmon, and mango barbecued mahi tacos. I opted for the more

conventional lobster roll and was happy with my choice. It had large chunks of fresh lobster with some capers sprinkled in and came on an authentic Maine-style roll, buttered and toasted. The Reef also does an extravagant Sunday brunch buffet, piled high with crab legs, peel-and-eat shrimp, and smoked salmon.

Central West

Of all the regions of Florida, none personifies the state's much varied culture and ethnicity as much as the Central West. From the Greek-settlement fishing-and-sponge-diving town of Tarpon Springs to Tampa's Cuban, Spanish, and Italian neighborhoods, to rural interior "Florida Cracker" communities like Cross Creek and Lake Panasoffkee, you will find it all here, and the influence on local cuisine has been profound. I hope you will pardon me if I sound a little biased and a bit long-winded in this section, but I've lived in Tampa my whole life, so this is my home turf and I'm proud of it.

* * *

Anna Maria

Rod and Reel Pier and Cafe, 875 North Shore Drive, Anna Maria 34216; (941) 778-1885; rodreelpier.com. The Rod and Reel Pier and Cafe, just around the northern point of Anna Maria Island, may be one of my favorite spots in all of Florida. It's also a place with great sentimental value to me. It's where I often ate lunch with my good friend and golfing buddy Andy Duncan, who passed away in 2014.

The Rod and Reel is a microcosm of everything that is both charming and sublimely quirky about coastal Florida. This 1947 2-story shack sits out on the end of the wooden pier and has a bait-and-tackle shop downstairs and a tiny short-order diner upstairs. Waves passing under the pier cause the wooden structure to creak and sway gently back and forth. Looking northwest, diners have a view of Passage Key and Egmont Key and the Gulf of Mexico beyond. To the northeast, you can see the Sunshine Skyway Bridge crossing the entrance to Tampa Bay. The Rod and Reel has one of the *better* grouper sandwiches on Florida's west coast, but it is the *best* place to eat one. Pelicans perch on the railings, patiently awaiting a fisherman's tossed treat. Manatees, dolphins, and stingrays routinely glide by beneath the pier. A raucous thunderstorm can blow up without any warning and then be gone just as quickly. If you're lucky, you might get to see a waterspout.

The Rod and Reel's fresh grouper sandwich comes fried, blackened, grilled, or Reuben. They also have oyster po'boys and crab cake sandwiches, plus full dinners of grouper, scallops, oysters, or crab cakes. Or if

Anna Maria: West Coast Getaway

Anna Maria Island has been a favorite getaway for west coast Floridians dating back to the early 1900s. Notwithstanding its prime location guarding the south entrance to Tampa Bay, and just offshore from Bradenton, Anna Maria manages to fend off the high-rise-condo and towering-hotel invasion to retain a relaxed-pace, beach-town flavor reminiscent of Florida's beach towns in the 1950s and '60s. And good eateries abound on Anna Maria Island, from bait-shop rustic to beachfront elegant.

you catch something off the pier that is plate-worthy, you might be able to talk the kitchen into cooking it up for you.

The Sandbar Restaurant, 100 Spring Avenue, Anna Maria 34216; (941) 778-0444; sandbar.groupersandwich.com. In 1979 Ed Chiles bought what first opened in 1946 as a small beachfront diner, converted out of an old Army barracks, and turned it into one of west coast Florida's most popular seafood restaurants. In the years since, he's added two more nearby: The Beach House in Bradenton Beach and Mar Vista on Longboat Key (see entries below). The Sandbar's regular menu includes enticing items like pan-seared crab-crusted sea scallops; shrimp Florentine with spinach, tomatoes, and white wine lemon-butter sauce over pasta; and a really good peel-and-eat Bud and Bay Shrimp (boiled in Budweiser and Old Bay seasoning) appetizer. The specials, like the crab-stuffed grouper, are always a good choice. When the weather is nice, the Sandbar will set up tables out on the beach sand, for true beachfront dining.

The Waterfront Restaurant, 111 South Bay Boulevard, Anna Maria 34216; (941) 778-1515; thewaterfrontrestaurant.net. Anna Maria Islanders Jason and Leah Suzor opened their Waterfront Restaurant in 1994 in a circa-1922 beach house with a wraparound porch. It sits just across the road from Anna Maria's City Pier (not to be confused with the Rod and Reel Pier), with a view across the mouth of Tampa Bay. Their predominantly seafood menu includes an assortment of flavorful appetizers like salmon smoked over applewood (they smoke it in-house) and the best grouper tacos on the island. Their main courses won't disappoint you either. Check out the Scallops Trovalo: pan-seared deep-sea scallops with mushrooms and roasted garlic, or the maple-mustard-crusted salmon, or the Brazilian *moqueca* stew with shrimp, clams, and fish in a coconut-lime broth.

Bartow

Catfish Country Restaurant, 2400 Griffin Road, Bartow 33830; (863) 646-6767; catfish-country.com. Look past the cartoon catfish characters on the sign and walls and the hokey references on the menu—"Bubba's Broiler," "Huck Finn's Sandwiches"—and you'll find some good seafood here. Obviously catfish is the specialty, and they do a fine job with it. Nearly all restaurant catfish is locally farm-raised these days, as is Catfish Country's. I had a Bubba's Broiler 4 Piece Catfish dinner. It came with 4 fillets on the plate they were broiled in, seasoned with lemon-pepper and parsley. The "Country" part is the sides: buttermilk biscuits, collard greens, cheese grits, and black eyed peas. They also serve farm-raised alligator, frog legs, crab cakes, and something they call Southern Pride Sharpies: fried whole catfish. The "Sharpies" probably refer to the sharp barbs in the catfish's dorsal and pectoral fins, or maybe it's just a warning to watch out for bones.

Bradenton and Bradenton Beach

The Beach House Restaurant, 200 Gulf Drive North, Bradenton Beach 34217; (941) 779-2222; beachhouse.groupersandwich.com. The Beach House is Ed Chiles's (see "The Sandbar Restaurant" in the Anna Maria section) latest. Like the Sandbar, it is right on the beach, and it offers a similar menu with perhaps a tad more casual atmosphere. It's a perfect, relaxing spot to enjoy your grouper sandwich, or maybe the mullet fingers dusted in cornmeal and fried, or grilled chimichurri (Argentinean pesto) tilefish.

Linger Lodge, 7205 85th Street Court East, Bradenton 34202; (941) 755-2757; lingerlodgeresort.com. Linger Lodge overlooks a tree-shaded bend in the Braden River, east of Bradenton. It began as a fishing camp campground back in the mid-1940s. Then in 1968 Frank and Elaine Gamsky moved down from Milwaukee, Wisconsin, and decided to buy the place. The Gamskys turned the lodge into a restaurant and opted to leave the surrounding campground in place. It's still there today. To get to the restaurant, you'll wind your way through campers and RVs. In 2005 former Florida State Senator Mike Bennett bought it from the Gamskys.

Linger Lodge's specialty is authentic Florida Cracker cuisine: catfish, gator tail, frog legs, and other local varmints. There is also a "Road Kill" section on the menu offering "Anything Dead on Bread," with some stomach-churning choices like Awesome 'Possum, Chunk of Skunk, Centerline Bovine, and Rigor Mortis Tortoise. Don't worry, it's a joke. But the gator ribs and the garlic-herb-butter-sautéed frog legs on the regular menu are real. As good as the food is, Linger Lodge's top attraction is their eclectic taxidermy decor, Frank Gamsky's handiwork. There is the obligatory jackalope, plus bobcats, coyotes, raccoons, a plethora of snakes, and, naturally, alligators. In 2003 Al Roker famously declared Linger Lodge "One of the top five weirdest restaurants in America," and I think he got it right.

Clearwater and Clearwater Beach

Frenchy's Original Cafe, 41 Baymont Street, Clearwater 33767; (727) 446-3607. **Frenchy's Rockaway Grill on the Beach,** 7 Rockaway Street, Clearwater 33767; (727) 461-4844. **Frenchy's Saltwater Cafe,** 419 Poinsettia Avenue, Clearwater 33767; (727) 461-6295. **Frenchy's South Beach Cafe,** 351 South Gulfview Boulevard, Clearwater 33767; (727) 461-9991. **Frenchy's Outpost Bar & Grill,** 466 Causeway Boulevard, Dunedin 34698; (727) 286-6139; frenchysonline.com. Québec, Canada, born Michael Preston grew up in Ann Arbor, Michigan, and then made his way to Clearwater Beach as a teenager in 1974, looking for whatever work he could find. Preston waited tables, washed dishes, and tended bars at the local tourist restaurants. It gave him a taste for what he would soon be applying to what would become one of Clearwater's most successful restaurants. Because of his Québec connection, his friends called him Frenchy.

In 1981 he rented a tiny corner cafe a block off the beach and opened the original Frenchy's Cafe. Soon he had to change the name to Frenchy's Original Cafe because he was opening additional locations (there are now five). Frenchy's formula was simple: generous servings of very fresh seafood and burgers, with a very casual beach ambience, and a friendly bar that served tropical drinks. Although he had burgers on the menu first, it was Frenchy's grouper sandwich that brought droves of customers through the door. While McDonald's Filet-o-Fish sandwich dates back to 1962, I'm pretty sure it never contained grouper. Most credit Michael "Frenchy" Preston with, if not inventing it, at least widely popularizing the grouper sandwich. The Frenchy's formula remains the same, and the grouper sandwich is still the no. 1 draw.

The original Frenchy's grouper sandwich came fried (not in oil but in butter) and with cheese on top, unless you specified otherwise. In addition, Frenchy's now offers their grouper sandwich grilled, Cajun (blackened seasoning), Reuben (with sauerkraut, Swiss cheese, and Thousand Island dressing), and buffalo (buffalo wing sauce, hot or mild). As popular as the grouper sandwiches are, it's easy to overlook the rest of their menu, which offers some other outstanding seafood dishes like orange-ginger snapper and shrimp scampi. They change the menu regularly according to what's fresh that day. In order to best facilitate that, they decided to integrate vertically. Frenchy's now owns its own seafood company, with a fleet of boats, and its own stone crab company as well.

Island Way Grill, 20 Island Way, Clearwater 33767; (727) 461-6617; islandwaygrill.com. Clearwater Memorial Causeway connects downtown Clearwater with Clearwater Beach, but halfway across you can stop at Pasadees Key. It's gotten busier in recent years because this is home to the Clearwater Marine Aquarium and the famous movie dolphin Winter. Next door to the aquarium, you'll find the casual-elegant Island Way Grill, opened by Clearwater restaurateur Frank Chivas and Baystar Restaurant Group in 2001. Their list of featured entrees includes pepper-crusted tuna with a teriyaki glaze, and salmon en papillote with jasmine rice and an assortment of Asian vegetables to give it an Oriental twist. They also have an inventive selection of small plates and appetizers, two of which I happily vouch for: a tangy tuna ceviche steeped in ginger, soy, lime, jalapeño, cilantro, and grape seed oil; and their Seafood Regatta, a marvelous bowl of scallops, shrimp, crab, and shiitake mushrooms in a rich herb-butter sauce. And Island Way Grill's Sunday brunch buffet is a

grand affair with lots of fresh seafood, a sushi bar, oysters on the half shell, shrimp, and smoked salmon.

Marlin Darlin Key West Grill, 2819 West Bay Drive, Clearwater 33770; (727) 584-1700; marlindarlinkeywestgrill.com. It's the name that hooks you (yes, pun intended) the first time. "Marlin Darlin" sounds like something you'd hear in a Conway Twitty song. It's the food that brings you back though. I had their excellent wood-fire-grilled scallops with bacon, spinach, pine nuts, and tomatoes over jasmine rice. They always have a daily selection of fresh catches, prepared in an assortment of ways, but wood-fire grilling is their specialty. Other dinner entrees include a terrific sesame-seared yellowfin tuna, a bodacious barbecued salmon, soft-shell crab, and lobster tempura. For lunch, try the tacos: grilled grouper, blackened tuna, fried hogfish, fried shrimp, or lobster tempura. Marlin Darlin also has one of the better key lime pies I've had. Frank Chivas (same owner as Island Way Grill, above) opened Marlin Darlin in Clearwater's upscale Belleair Bluffs in 2006.

Ward's Seafood Market, 1001 Belleair Road, Clearwater 33756; (727) 518-8701; wardsseafood.com. Millie and Johnny Ward had been selling fresh-caught fish out of a street-side pushcart when they decided to open Ward's Seafood Market back in 1955. It's been a Clearwater Belleair neighborhood fixture ever since. Ward's was sold twice, once in 1975 to Wayne Widmark, then again in 1990 to current owner Rob Cameron, whom Widmark had hired to manage it 4 years earlier. The Wards had set a high standard for quality and freshness, only buying from a select group of local fishermen. Subsequent owners have done an outstanding job of maintaining that reputation. Also, you can order over the counter baskets of fresh shrimp, oysters, salmon, mullet, or scallops, or a variety of fresh fish sandwiches—mahi, mullet, amberjack, catfish, or grouper—to eat at one of the 4 small tables in one corner of the market. Ward's Grilled Grouper Sandwich ranks as one of the very best I've had anywhere, and I've been eating a lot of grouper sandwiches!

Cortez

Star Fish Company Market and Restaurant, 12306 46th Avenue West, Cortez 34215; (941) 794-1243; starfishcompany.com. Star Fish Company is one of those Cortez commercial seafood businesses that started back in the early 1920s. In the 1960s they added a small retail market. Then in 1996 Karen Bell bought the business and decided to put some picnic tables on the dock out back and sell fish sandwiches. Essentially Karen has been in the business her entire life. Her grandfather Aaron Bell started the A. B. Bell Fish Company (next door) in 1940, and she runs that now too. Star Fish Company Restaurant is still just picnic tables on the dock behind the market, except there are more of them. It's cash-only, and whatever you order will be served in a cardboard box. The food—grouper, oysters, shrimp, mullet, pompano, crab cakes, shrimp or oyster po'boys, and conch fritters—is fantastic. Seafood is always that much fresher (and tastes that much better) when it just came off one your own boats that morning.

Tide Tables at Marker 48, 12507 Cortez Road West, Cortez 34215; (941) 567-6206; facebook.com/tidetables. In 2013 Karen Bell (see "Star Fish Company Market and Restaurant" above), along with business partners Bobby and Gwen Woodson, opened a second Cortez restaurant, Tide Tables (at Channel Marker 48), next to the Cortez Bridge, just a

few blocks away from Star Fish Company. Same great seafood fresh off Star Fish Company's boats; and same great old-Florida-fishing-village atmosphere but with a little extra elbow room. I opted for their Combo Basket, with mahi, scallops, and shrimp, all blackened, and it was excellent. You can tell a difference between fresh just out of the water this morning and fresh from 2 days ago, and this was the former. I ate at the outdoor bar and it seems to me that Tide Tables might even be a bit more of a locals place than Star Fish. Everybody there knew everybody else, except me.

Cortez: True Fishing Village

Cortez may be the last of something once commonplace in yesterday's Florida: a coastal commercial fishing village. Everything in Cortez is somehow related to seafood, fishing, or boats. Simple clapboard cottages, many dating back to the 1920s, make up the quiet neighborhood surrounding the boat docks and fish warehouses that line the shoreline along Anna Maria Sound. In the mid-1800s it was known as Hunter's Point, but locals called it "the Kitchen" because of the abundance of seafood and shellfish caught in these waters.

Cross Creek

The Yearling Restaurant, 14531 County Road 325, Cross Creek 32640; (352) 466-3999; yearlingrestaurant.net. When Ben Wheeler opened the Yearling Restaurant in 1952, it was one of the first genuine "Florida Cracker cuisine" restaurants, serving such rural fare as frog legs, gator tail, catfish, fried quail, collard greens, and turtle. It closed in 1992, but then local Citra resident Robert Blaur bought it and reopened in 2002. Thankfully, Blaur

Marjorie Rawlings

Cross Creek is a quiet little place, situated between Orange and Lochloosa Lakes, about 22 miles south of Gainesville. Pulitzer Prize–winning author Marjorie Rawlings lived here and wrote books and short stories about life in rural north-central Florida in the 1930s and '40s. Her most famous were *The Yearling* and *Cross Creek*. Rawlings's circa-1890 Cross Creek home and the surrounding property are now the Marjorie Kinnan Rawlings State Historic Site, an absolute must-visit if you are a fan of her writing.

decided to keep the Yearling's original ambience, and most importantly its authentic cuisine, intact. Even the restaurant's original 1970s–'80s head chef Junior Jenkins came back. Nothing beats consuming a heaping plate of plump fried frog legs while listening to bona fide blues guitarist Willie Green belt out "Kansas City Here I Come." And the only place where you can enjoy both at the same time is the Yearling. On my most recent visit, I ordered the frog legs, the fattest I've ever seen. They were the size of chicken legs and just as meaty. By the way, the old adage about "it tastes like chicken" is true with frog legs: similar flavor, just a bit chewier.

Crystal River and Ozello

Charlie's Fish House Restaurant and Seafood Market, 224 US Highway 19, Crystal River 34428; (352) 795-3949 (restaurant); (352) 795-2468 (market); charliesfishhouse.com. From the back deck at Charlie's Fish House, I watched a school of 6-foot-long tarpons rolling along the seawall in the Crystal River. With their large protruding lower jaws and giant silvery scales, they look almost prehistoric. You can't eat them, but they are fascinating to watch. Since tarpon is not on the menu, I had Charlie's stewed oysters in a tangy tomato broth, with grits and hush puppies. Charlie and Marion Kofmehl opened their seafood market and restaurant here in 1960, and in the early 1970s, sons Jimmy and Phil took over. In 1990 they built the current restaurant and consolidated the market under the same roof. Charlie's expansive menu includes items like

crabmeat-stuffed turbot; salmon Oscar with lump crab, asparagus, and béarnaise sauce on top of a fresh Atlantic salmon fillet; and steak Oscar, which does the same on top of filet mignon.

Dan's Clam Stand, 2315 North Sunshine Path, Crystal River 34428; (352) 795-9081; kingclam.com. Captain Dan Cyr got his start as a lobster fisherman in Cape Cod before moving to Florida, where he opened Dan's Clam Stand alongside Highway 44, the "Gulf to Lake Highway" in Crystal River. Obviously their specialty is fresh clams, and I had a big basket of fried "whole belly" clams that were juicy and filling.

Peck's Old Port Cove Seafood Restaurant and Blue Crab Farm, 139 North Ozello Trail, Crystal River 34429; (352) 795-2806. About halfway between Crystal River and Homosassa, Citrus County Road 494, also called Ozello Trail, winds west for about 9 miles through swampy forest and palmetto scrub. Intermittently, as you near the coast, the road opens up to saw grass savannas dotted with cedar bay heads. The community of Ozello is technically on an island, separated from the mainland by tributaries of the St. Martin River, Salt Creek, and Greenleaf Bay. Hundreds of water passageways crosshatch this nether land. Airboats are the transport of choice here.

Seafood Lover's Florida

Ozello Trail ends where it runs into the open Gulf of Mexico and at Peck's Old Port Cove Seafood Restaurant and Blue Crab Farm. Calvin Peck began harvesting blue crabs in specially constructed tanks behind his restaurant here in 1982. I've eaten at Peck's many times, usually when I had a craving for a heaping bowl of their steaming garlic crabs. They'll give you a bib, and you'll need it, but you're going to get splattered with crab shell, butter, and garlic anyway. Granted, the ratio of crabmeat-acquired to work-cracking-to-get-it is low, but it is so worth it.

Dunedin

Frenchy's Outpost Bar & Grill, 466 Causeway Boulevard, Dunedin 34698; (727) 286-6139; frenchysonline.com. See main listing on p. 68.

Pinellas Trail

The Pinellas Trail, built along 34 miles of abandoned CSX railroad right-of-way from St. Petersburg to Tarpon Springs, is one of the most successful and popular Rails-to-Trails projects in the country. Pinellas County Parks and Recreation estimates that 90,000 people use it each month.

When word came that the Pinellas Trail would open up through downtown Dunedin, north of Clearwater, in 1991, the town recognized a golden opportunity. What was once a nuisance (a railroad crossing right in the middle of their downtown) would become an attraction, drawing new potential customers—walkers, joggers, bicyclists, and inline skaters—into a waning district. Dunedin's Community Redevelopment Agency quickly went to work on plans to revitalize Main Street, with the Pinellas Trail's crossing as its centerpiece. The result has been a resounding success. Downtown Dunedin is now a lively pedestrian-friendly district with tree-lined brick walkways, restaurants, galleries, and shops. A couple of the restaurants actually front on the trail itself. The Pinellas Trail–Main Street crossing is now an inviting gathering spot with park benches, parklike landscaping, and colorful outdoor sculptures.

The Salty Dawg, 941 Huntley Avenue, Dunedin 34698; (727) 735-0498; saltydawgdunedin.com. Follow the Pinellas Trail a couple blocks north of Main Street and you will reach the Salty Dawg, a Key-Westy bar and grill. Their back deck has a gate that opens directly onto the trail. Menu items include lobster egg rolls, grouper or shrimp tacos, fried oyster or shrimp baskets, and of course grouper sandwiches.

Dunnellon

Blue Gator Tiki Bar and Restaurant, 12189 South Williams Street, Dunnellon 34432; (352) 465-1635; blue-gator.com. The open-air Blue Gator Tiki Bar overlooks a bend in the picturesque Withlacoochee River. They offer an assortment of fried baskets including grouper fingers, oysters, scallops, and frog legs, but I ordered a pound of peel-and-eat shrimp, generously seasoned and delicious. It does seem to taste a little better when you're eating it alongside the banks of one of Florida's most scenic rivers.

Gulfport

Backfin Blue Cafe, 2913 Beach Boulevard South, Gulfport 33707; (727) 343-2583; backfinbluecafe.com. Backfin Blue Cafe occupies a quaint tree-shaded 1927 bungalow on Beach Boulevard in St. Petersburg artist community Gulfport. Original paintings from local neighborhood artists hang on the walls. Diners can eat inside or outside on the porch. I always start with a bowl of chef and owner Harold Russell's hearty, savory Corn

Interview with Harold Russell,
Chef and Owner Backfin Blue Cafe

Backfin Blue Cafe owner and chef Harold Russell learned his earliest lessons about the seafood restaurant business at his grandfather Harold Blum's restaurant in West Keansburg, New Jersey. Freshness was lesson no. 1.

"Grandpa would actually set his own traps and catch his own seafood," Harold recalls. "Whatever he served was what he had caught down on 'the Shore' that morning. When Grandpa would catch blue crabs, he'd put them in a pen. My brothers, cousins, and I liked it when the soft shells were running because we could play with those without getting pinched."

Those memories appear to have had a lasting influence. Harold has spent much of his life designing recipes and preparing great food. He ran the kitchen at the Hurricane Restaurant on Pass-a-Grille for 13 years and was a chef at Shula's Steakhouse in Tampa as well. But what he really wanted was his own place. "I was actually looking for a downtown location near Tropicana Field when an ad popped up in the paper for this cottage in Gulfport."

Harold opened Backfin Blue Cafe in 1997. "Backfin Blue" refers to blue crabs. Harold's signature dish is his melt-in-your-mouth Maryland-style jumbo lump blue-crab cakes. Like everything on the menu, they are baked, not fried. "Everything we cook is actually out of one oven, an old-fashioned convection oven. No real secret to our crab recipe. Start out by buying the best and freshest crabs. By baking them, we can use very little filler (and more lump crab)."

Harold's famous Corn and Crab Chowder started out as a Cajun recipe. "It was really hot," he explains, "so I played with the seasoning some." He ended up with less hot pepper and more Old Bay seasoning, which they use in a lot of their dishes. Rows of empty Old Bay tins line the rafter above the restaurant's cozy bar.

Harold was happy to share a recipe for one of his "regular specials" with me. "I like coming up with recipes that people can do at home, like my herb-crusted salmon." To see Harold's recipe, go to the "In the Kitchen" section at the back of the book.

and Crab Chowder. His specials change daily. On my most recent visit, the special was crab-stuffed shrimp with fire-roasted red pepper cream sauce that was spectacular. Here are some other mouthwatering appetizer treats: lobster ravioli with that same sauce; crab martini—jumbo lump crab with cilantro, guacamole, corn salsa, and tortilla chips; and bacon-wrapped, basil-stuffed, barbecued shrimp. And then there is Harold's rightful claim to fame: his outstanding baked Maryland-style jumbo lump blue-crab cakes.

Fish Bar and Grille, 3038 Beach Boulevard, Gulfport 33707; (727) 328-2720; fishbarandgrillegulfport.com. Gulfport, a waterfront neighborhood nestled on Boca Ciega Bay, has long been known for its arts-and-crafts galleries and shops. More recently it has added "culinary destination" to that reputation. Along its 3-block-long main street, Beach Boulevard, you'll find excellent Italian, Brazilian, and Greek cuisine, and of course outstanding seafood. Gulfport's newest seafood restaurant, Fish Bar and Grille, has a casual, tropical, Polynesian vibe. Most diners sit outside under umbrellas among flowers and palm trees in the garden that surrounds an

Arts and Crafts–era bungalow (where there is also indoor seating). Mike and Cathy Burke opened Fish Bar and Grille in March 2016. Their menu includes fresh-caught grouper and snapper with a choice of sauces: citrus teriyaki, mango-pineapple, or soy honey-ginger lime. There's also steamed clams, steamed or fried oysters, oyster or shrimp po'boys, grouper, snapper, and crab cake sandwiches, plus some enticing appetizers like ahi tuna nachos, shrimp and scallop ceviche, and a very flavorful sweet Hawaiian-style ahi tuna poke, with cubed raw tuna, scallions, and citrus ponzu sauce, served with jasmine rice and wakame (seaweed)—which I had for an appetizer. For a main course I opted for their savory lobster roll sandwich, which was stuffed with fresh lobster tail and claw meat.

Neptune Grill, 5501 Shore Boulevard, Gulfport 33707; (727) 623-4823; neptunegrillgulfport.com. With the Greek community of Tarpon Springs close by (see Tarpon Springs entries), there has always been a significant Greek influence on local food. Greek diners can be found throughout the greater St. Petersburg–Tampa-Clearwater area, and Neptune Grill is a fine example of one of these. Seafood features prominently in the Greek diet, and thus it also does on Greek restaurants' menus. Neptune Grill offers grilled octopus and fried calamari, along with fried shrimp, bacon-wrapped scallops and shrimp, and Maryland crab cakes as appetizers. For

entrees they do a larger portion of the Maryland crab cakes, crabmeat-stuffed flounder, and seafood Mediterranean pasta with shrimp, scallops, and grouper topped with green peppers, spinach, garlic, tomatoes, and kalamata olives. I tried their Greek-style grouper, which is baked in lemon, butter, and olive oil, then topped with oregano, garlic, pepper, and parsley. It's a simple, timeless, and classic Greek preparation that works beautifully.

Save on Seafood Market, 1449 49th Street South, Gulfport 33707; (727) 323-0155; saveonseafoodmarket.com. Save on Seafood Market has been South St. Petersburg's and Gulfport's go-to market for the best selection of fresh fish since opening in 1981. They have fresh-cut fillets of grouper and mahi, plus flown-in-fresh Chilean sea bass, cod, Dover sole, and New Zealand salmon. But wild locally caught whole fish makes up their largest selection: red snapper, grouper, flounder, hogfish, mullet, sheepshead, and porgy are all regular items, in addition to fresh shrimp, oysters, and crabs.

Spinnakers, 3128 Beach Boulevard, Gulfport 33707; (727) 350-5903; beachhausrestaurant.com. Spinnakers' dog-friendly (Gulfport is a very dog-friendly town) rooftop deck bar has the best view across Boca Ciega Bay in Gulfport. Their dining room is downstairs, but the menu is the same up on the roof, and if the weather is nice, why not? They also have a terrific seafood selection, and at least one item I've never found anywhere else, a seafood-stuffed pepper. It's a large green bell pepper stuffed with crabmeat, crawfish meat, shrimp, fish, and rice, then baked and served with marinara sauce. It was wonderful! This is an idea that I'm surprised hasn't caught on elsewhere. My dining companion Nancy Pepper had their mahimahi, rubbed with blackening seasoning and then char-grilled, also delicious. Other seafood main courses include seared sea scallops wrapped in bacon and jalapeños; grouper (fried, blackened, or grilled) topped with roasted red peppers, onions, and fried okra; Ruby's Fried Catfish with grit cakes and a fried egg; shrimp scampi; fish-and-chips; and something they call Boca Bay Pasta, with shrimp, crawfish, crab, whitefish, and andouille sausage, tossed in angel-hair pasta, with pepper and tomato sauce.

Holmes Beach

Beach Bistro, 6600 Gulf Drive, Holmes Beach 34217; (941) 778-6444; beachbistro.com. Restaurateurs Sean and Susan Murphy came to Holmes Beach, on the south end of Anna Maria Island, and opened Beach

Bistro in 1985. The Murphys arrived by way of New Orleans, where Sean worked at Arnaud's. Beach Bistro is a tiny place right on the beach, much understated from the outside but very elegant on the inside. With limited seating, a reservation is a must. Their two regular grouper dishes qualify as exceptional: cashew-and-coconut-crusted Floribbean Grouper and Grouper Cooper, which is pan-seared with a poached lobster tail. But Sean's savory Bistro Bouillabaisse may be the king of the Beach Bistro menu.

Eat Here, 5315 Gulf Drive, Holmes Beach 34217; (941) 778-0411; eathereflorida.com. Also 240 Avenida Madera, Siesta Key 34242; (941) 346-7800; eathereflorida.com. Sean Murphy's (see "Beach Bistro" above) newest venture, Eat Here, has two locations, one in Holmes Beach and one in Siesta Key. Eat Here takes a much more casual approach to ambience, as well as the menu, than Beach Bistro, but still applies the same perfectionist attention to the quality and preparation of the food. I went to the Holmes Beach restaurant and decided to try something that sounded casual (and ultimately tasted terrific): grilled lobster-and-shrimp tacos with a garlic, butter, and lime sauce. My dining companion Nancy had one of the day's specials: Cajun dusted deep-sea scallops with melon jam and a sweet pear-and-grape chutney. I managed to get my fork into a couple of Nancy's scallops and they were outstanding, worthy of Beach Bistro any day. So, you can get tacos and pizza at Eat Here, but you can also get oven-roasted Atlantic salmon with horseradish cream sauce, fire-roasted clams in white wine and garlic butter, and Eat Here's version of bouillabaisse, Gulf Coast seafood stew with fresh catch-of-the-day fish, shrimp, clams, mussels, and andouille sausage.

Homosassa

The Freezer Tiki Bar, 5590 South Boulevard Drive, Homosassa 34448; (352) 628-2452; facebook.com/pages/The-Freezer/ 497426656936992. The first time I drove by the Freezer I didn't stop because I thought it was a wholesale seafood warehouse, and it is. But if you walk up the ramp and through the freezer curtain, you suddenly find yourself in one of this area's worst-kept secrets. The Freezer Tiki Bar backs up to a creek that veers off of the Homosassa River. There's a thatch roof over the top, but it's all open-air. It's also cash-only. Everything is fresh: steamed peel-and-eat shrimp, steamed blue crabs, stone crab claws (when they're in season, mid-October to mid-May), and one of my favorites, smoked mullet.

Indian Rocks Beach

Guppy's on the Beach Seafood Grill & Bar, 1701 Gulf Boulevard, Indian Rocks Beach 33785; (727) 593-2032; 3bestchefs.com/guppys. Guppy's is another seafood restaurant from Mystic Fish (see Palm Harbor section) owner Eugene Fuhrmann. The atmosphere is beach-casual, befitting Indian Rocks, and the food is top-notch. In the appetizer section of the menu, two notables are the truffle lobster mac-and-cheese and the Greek-style char-grilled octopus with feta cheese, kalamata olives, and tomato dill coulis. For entrees I like their hoisin-lacquered sea bass and their pan-fried grouper (or snapper) piccata with lemon-caper-butter sauce. I had a marvelous special of the day: Margate snapper crusted with Asiago cheese and smothered with a creamed-leeks sauce. They also offer some other interesting entrees, like potato-crusted salmon, Clear Springs rainbow trout with panko crust, char-grilled bacon-wrapped swordfish, and lobster ravioli.

Lake Panasoffkee

Catfish Johnny's, 2396 North Highway 470, Lake Panasoffkee 33538; (352) 793-2083; catfishjohnnysrestaurant.com. Patricia and John "Catfish Johnny" Galvin opened Catfish Johnny's in 2002. It's a place known for their local fresh catfish, perch, and gator baskets, but perhaps it's even better known because it is owned by longtime popular country musician Johnny Galvin. Lake Panasoffkee is a tiny and close-knit, off-the-beaten-path community, and Catfish Johnny's is a regular hangout for locals, both for the good food and the warm company. I enjoyed my fried perch basket, along with some friendly conversation with people who had never met me but treated me like an old friend.

Longboat Key

Mar Vista Dockside Restaurant, 760 Broadway Street, North Longboat Key 34228; (941) 383-2391; marvista.groupersandwich.com. Mar Vista is my favorite of Ed Chiles's three restaurants. Not just because the food is great, as it also is at his other restaurants, but because of Mar Vista's character and history. Shorefront outdoor seating in the shade of old twisted oaks surrounds what was once an old bait shop and bar, built in 1913 by early Longboat Key developer Rufus Jordan. It's one of the oldest

structures on Longboat Key. In fisherman's-bar tradition, dollar bills grace the ceiling and walls. Fishermen used to write their names on a dollar bill and then tack it on a bar's wall. That way, if they were broke the next time they came in, they'd have something to buy a drink with. I had Mar Vista's marvelous blackened mullet tacos, made with local Cortez mullet and garnished with sweet slaw. There are other enticing items on the menu too, like Bud and Bay Peel-and-Eat Shrimp, same as at the Sandbar; plus some special items like Red Curry Red Snapper with a Thai-style curry, coconut, and cilantro sauce, and Shrimp with Cortez Bottarga. Bottarga is salt-cured, sun-dried mullet roe, and Ed Chiles is a partner in the Anna Maria Fish Company that produces it.

Madeira Beach

Dockside Dave's, 14701 Gulf Boulevard, Madeira Beach 33708; (727) 392-9399; docksidedavesgrill.com. Dockside Dave's opened in Madeira Beach in 1978 and is the proverbial hole-in-the-wall dive, a locals' hangout with great food. In my estimation, Dockside Dave's contends for best grouper sandwich on the beach. It's certainly the biggest. This is a sandwich that you have to eat with a fork and knife. Remember Wendy's "Where's the beef?" ad campaign from the 1980s? Well, the question for Dave's is "Where's the bun?" because it's hidden underneath a half-pound grouper fillet. Dave's will make their "Famous" fish sandwich beer-batter fried, blackened, lemon-pepper grilled, or Buffalo-style.

Friendly Fisherman, 150 Boardwalk Place, Madeira Beach 33708; (727) 391-6025; gofriendlyfisherman.com. There are some St. Pete Beach seafood tourist restaurants that have stood the test of time. The Friendly Fisherman at John's Pass is one. The family patriarch Captain Wilson "Hub" Hubbard's parents were in the traveling-carnival business, but in 1929 they came to Pass-a-Grille (the south end of St. Pete Beach) and stayed. They started a bait-and-day-fishing-trip business, which evolved into a larger fishing-charter business that still operates today. There were other side businesses along the way too, including a live porpoise show back in the 1950s (long before SeaWorld). And for many decades Wilson Hubbard was the host of a popular radio show about fishing. In 1976 Hubbard moved operations up the road to John's Pass, at Madeira Beach, and in 1978 opened the Friendly Fisherman. Today, I think it has a kind of kitschy, 1970s-nostalgia-tourist-spot feel, with a nice view of John's Pass

from the upper-level boardwalk. Among expected menu items like the Captains Platter (broiled or fried) with grouper, scallops, and shrimp, look for the less typical fresh-catch items for the day, like amberjack, swordfish, or sea bass. I'm also partial to their broiled Caribbean lobster tails.

Ocklawaha

Gator Joe's Beach Bar and Grill, 12431 Southeast 135th Avenue, Ocklawaha 32179; (352) 288-3100; gatorjoesocala.com. Gator Joe's Beach Bar and Grill pays tribute not to the Ma Barker Gang but to lovable Old

Ma Barker Gang

The quiet community of Ocklawaha wraps around the north shore of Lake Weir, about 20 miles southeast of Ocala. In the summertime Lake Weir is a popular waterskiing and fishing spot. Cabins and docks line the shore, and Gator Joe's Beach Bar and Grill, in an old 1926 stilt building, sits on the lake's edge. Gator Joe's is a great local's joint for Florida Cracker cuisine like frog legs, catfish sandwiches, and gator tail.

Waterskiing, fishing, and eating some good grub are usually about as exciting as things get around here. But 80 years ago, less than a quarter-mile down the beach from Gator Joe's, the reign of one of history's most infamous bank-robbery and kidnapping gangs ended in a bloody gun battle with the FBI. In the predawn hours of January 16, 1935, FBI agents caught up with the notorious Ma Barker Gang and then engaged in a 6-hour shootout that left Ma and son Fred dead.

When Ma and Fred Barker, under the alias "the Blackburns," first came to Ocklawaha in 1934, they were considered friendly by the locals. They were regulars and big tippers at the bar. But before long boredom got the best of Fred, and he began shooting at ducks on Lake Weir with his machine gun, and that did not set well with the locals. When Fred let it be known that he wanted to hunt down "Old Joe," a legendary (but considered harmless) old alligator that lived in the lake, the locals were enraged, and word of his intentions spread. His description matched one given by the FBI, and early on the morning of January 16, 14 agents surrounded the house. They fired over 1,500 rounds of bullets into the house in three-quarters of an hour and then continued to shoot through the windows intermittently for 5 more hours. When they finally went inside, they found Ma and Fred dead on the floor of the bullet-ridden upstairs bedroom. They also found an arsenal of rifles, machine guns, pistols, and ammunition. Ma was still clutching her machine gun in her hands.

Joe himself (his actual paw hangs on the wall), although gator tail does feature prominently on the menu, as do shrimp, clams, frog legs, Alaskan pollock, and mahimahi. All come fried, but you can get the mahi blackened or grilled. I sprung for the Gator Tail Basket—cubed bites of gator tail, lightly seasoned and fried.

Oldsmar

Jack Willie's Bar, Grill and Tiki, 1013 St. Petersburg Drive West, Oldsmar 34677; (813) 749-7932; jackwilliesbarandgrill.com. Veer off of busy Highway 580 in Oldsmar on St. Petersburg Drive and you'll find Jack Willie's, a thatched-roof oasis alongside Moccasin Creek. This is a great spot for viewing wildlife. Manatees, dolphins, and even alligators are frequent visitors in the creek, which spills into the north end of Tampa Bay just around the bend. When I visited we watched a very brave heron named Fred waltz up to one of the outdoor tables and grab the bun right off of a diner's sandwich. Fred, a fixture at Jack Willie's, knows the sandwiches here are terrific, particularly the grilled grouper or mahi. But if you want something a little different, try the Gator Sausage Hoagie. They also have fried oyster, shrimp, and grouper po'boys, a fried oyster burger, a crab cake sandwich, and fish-and-chips, plus crabmeat-stuffed shrimp, grilled salmon, and seafood combo platter dinners.

Ozona

Molly Goodhead's Raw Bar & Restaurant, 400 Orange Street, Ozona 34660; (727) 786-6255; mollygoodheads.com. She sounds like the female lead for a James Bond movie, but presumably Molly Goodhead is a mermaid. Owner Laurel Flowers opened Molly Goodhead's Raw Bar & Restaurant in 1985 in a circa-1919 house that belonged to the Stansells, a multi-generation pioneering family from this area. The catchy name brings customers into this Key West–casual eatery tucked away in Ozona, but it's the good food and fun atmosphere that brings them back. Their menu runs the full seafood gamut. Raw bar options and appetizers include raw oysters, steamed oysters, steamed clams, steamed mussels, steamed peel-and-eat shrimp, fried calamari, fried, blackened, or grilled gator tail, ahi tuna sushi martini, conch fritters, and grouper nuggets. And there are the more upscale entrees: char-grilled orange-honey-glazed salmon, panko-encrusted mahi with blueberry soy sauce, and crab-stuffed flounder. But perhaps their best item is Molly's Fresh off the Boat Grouper Sandwich, fried, blackened, or, my preference, char-grilled.

Palm Harbor

Mystic Fish, 3253 Tampa Road, Palm Harbor 34684; (727) 771-1800; 3bestchefs.com/mystic. From their eclectic menu to the whimsical interior, everything about Mystic Fish in Palm Harbor seems to defy categorization. "That's the way we wanted it," co-owner and chef Doug Bebell explained to me when I interviewed him for a *DuPont Registry* magazine article a few years back. "We don't follow the trends or label what we prepare." As for that interior, it could be Merlin the Magician's dining room. Rob "Fishbone" Goines, whom Bebell described as a "wandering bohemian interior designer," fashioned the decor that includes hand-built teak and fossil-stone-inlaid booth tables, a wall border made from Mexican abalone shells, spiraling horn sculptures made from movie film by Gulfport artist Nancy Cervenka, blown-glass sconces, and three tropical fish tanks. In addition, Goines created the restaurant's namesake and mascot, which resides on the stained-glass front door.

Bebell and business partner Eugene Fuhrmann (who also own Guppy's in Indian Rocks Beach; see "Indian Rocks Beach" entry) opened Mystic Fish in 2001. Their menu features flavors from the far-flung corners of the world but favors Asian and Italian. Savory seafood entrees include Chilean sea bass with a soy-hijiki sauce, Atlantic salmon with pistachio-dill pesto, and a superb saffron-rich bouillabaisse swimming with scallops, mussels, clams, lobster, and shrimp. And their Bermuda Fish Chowder is so good I can only describe it as transcendental.

Pinellas Park

Cajun Cafe on the Bayou, 8101 Park Boulevard, Pinellas Park 33781; (727) 546-6732; cajuncafeonthebayou.com. French Acadians, living in what is now southeastern Canada, had fought with the British for most of the first half of the 18th century. That conflict ultimately came to an end during the French and Indian War. In 1755 the British began deporting Acadians south in "Le Grand Dérangement." Many ended up in what is now Louisiana. "Acadian" became "Cajun," and that French influence on Louisiana culture, language, and, perhaps most importantly, food is legendary.

Traditionally, Cajun food has some kick, and that's what you'll find at Cajun Cafe on Cross Bayou in Pinellas Park. Joe Thibodaux (from Thibodaux, Louisiana) opened the cafe in 1996 and put lots of spicy dishes, like jambalaya, red beans and rice, and gumbo, on the menu. He also added traditional Cajun seafood entrees like frog legs (that's right, I'm calling frog legs "seafood"), catfish, Cajun popcorn (crawfish), and soft-shell crab. When Joe retired in 2003, his daughter Rebecca and her husband Paul Unwin took over. They added an extensive craft beer list to the menu and kept the Cajun cuisine exactly the same.

Seafood Lover's Florida

Redington Beach

Conch Republic, 10099 Gulf Boulevard, Redington Beach 33708; (727) 320-0536; conchrepublicgrill.com. Conch Republic looks like the typical beach-tourist seafood joint: a T-shirt shop at the entrance, crab trap light fixtures, old service station signs hanging from the ceiling, and the requisite Jimmy Buffet soundtrack. But they do a good job with seafood. Conch Republic buys their fresh fish whole and fillets them in-house, assuring that they are as fresh as possible. Try the grouper Reuben. It's "New York deli" meets "Florida fish shack." They also do terrific fish tacos and a savory cedar-plank-baked salmon.

Sarasota

The Columbia Restaurant, 411 St. Armands Circle, Sarasota 34236; (941) 388-3987; columbiarestaurant.com. See main listing on p. 115.

John Ringling: The Circus and the Arts

Much of Sarasota's history centers around one person, John Ringling, the man who brought the circus to town. But his influence on Sarasota extended way beyond the big top. Ringling was one of five brothers who started a circus business in 1884. John was in charge of transport. Within a few years he had converted the show from wagons to railroad, greatly expanding their reach and propelling the circus's growth. In 1906 and 1907 they bought out two competitors, including Barnum & Bailey.

John and Mable Ringling had made their home in Sarasota, although the circus's main headquarters were in Bridgeport, Connecticut. With Florida's popularity on the rise, Ringling saw Sarasota's great potential as a summer resort town. In 1922 and 1923 he purchased a string of barrier islands, including St. Armands Key, Lido Key, Bird Key, and the south end of Longboat Key, intent on developing a resort community called Ringling Isles. Then in 1924 he built the bridge from downtown Sarasota to St. Armands Key. The following year he and Mable constructed their colossal 32-room Venetian Gothic home on Sarasota Bay, which they named Ca'd' Zan, "House of John." But then in 1926, Florida land values began to nosedive, and Ringling decided to move the entire Ringling Bros. and Barnum & Bailey Circus from Connecticut down to Sarasota in an effort to revitalize the local economy. It paid off. Sarasota weathered the late 1920s better than the rest of Florida.

While the circus, the railroad, and property development were Ringling's professional pursuits, collecting art was his passion. John and Mable were frequent travelers to Europe and particularly fond of Italy. They collected a considerable amount of art and furnishings from there and abroad. In 1927, on the grounds of Ca'd' Zan, they established the John and Mable Ringling Museum of Art, but it was not completed until 1929, sadly, the year Mable died.

With the Florida land-boom crash followed by the 1929 stock market crash, and Mable's death that same year, John Ringling had suffered a barrage of personal and financial blows. He died in 1936 almost completely drained of his fortune; however, he left an indelible mark on Sarasota. He was the town's foremost developer and its most ardent advocate, almost single-handedly setting the tone for the cultural atmosphere that Sarasota is known for today. In the end, of all that he had accumulated and lost, it was his passionate pursuit of art, not his business investments, that retained the most value. Today the Ringling Museum of Art houses the Ringlings' collection of over 600 paintings, many 16th- and 17th-century Italian and Flemish Baroque, including an outstanding selection of Peter Paul Rubens works, one of Ringling's favorites.

Crab & Fin, 20 St. Armands Circle, Sarasota 34236; (941) 388-3964; crabfinrestaurant.com. Jim and Pam MacDonald opened Charley's Crab, one of my longtime favorites, on Sarasota's trendy St. Armands Circle back in 1978. It was a franchise, and there were five in Florida. When the Landry's Restaurants Group bought out the franchise in 2002, the MacDonalds decided to open their own restaurant, Crab & Fin, at the same location. Their son Scott runs it today. Crab & Fin has an even more extensive menu than Charley's Crab had, with a raw bar that specializes in fresh oysters from a variety of locations: British Columbia Fanny Bays, Nova Scotia Tatamagouches, Prince Edward Island Summersides, Massachusetts Riptides, Connecticut Blue Points, and Rhode Island Beaver Tails. They can be ordered individually or mixed-and-matched as a sampler. Entrees include pan-seared Scottish salmon, sesame-crusted rare

yellowfin tuna, and blackened grouper tacos, among others. My charbroiled swordfish with shrimp and smoked bacon grits was excellent.

Owen's Fish Camp, 516 Burns Lane, Sarasota 34236; (941) 951-6936; owensfishcamp.com. "Owen" is Owen Burns, who came from Maryland to Sarasota in 1910, when it was still a backwater town. He began buying up and developing the property that is now Sarasota's downtown and surrounding neighborhoods. He was also instrumental in the development of St. Armands Key, Lido Key, and Longboat Key, and even constructed John and Mable Ringling's Ca'd' Zan, although a subsequent failed property-development partnership with Ringling would ultimately leave him bankrupt.

Reportedly, Burns was an avid fisherman, and that might be why he came to Sarasota originally. So Owen's Fish Camp, in a banyan-tree-shaded circa-1920s bungalow on Burns Lane, is an ode to both Burns and to the Sarasota that he found when he first arrived. The Caragiulo Brothers are synonymous with great restaurants in Sarasota. They own Shore Diner on St. Armands Key, Nancy's Barbecue, and Caragiulo's Italian Restaurant, and they opened Owen's Fish Camp in 2010. It features a seafood-centric menu with an old-Florida slant. Among the starter items are Bloody Mary oyster shooters and chicken-fried lobster tail, which I ordered and loved! For my entree I had their catch-of-the-day grilled tripletail with lemon and

Seafood for Vegans?

Can seaweed be seafood? Why not? It comes from the sea. If you're a sushi fan (as I am), you've probably consumed nori. Sushi crafters use it as the outer layer of a sushi roll, mostly just to hold it together but for flavor too. Nori is made from a red algae seaweed (that's actually more purplish-green) that's chopped up, dried, and pressed into thin paper-like sheets. It's also used to flavor Japanese soups and noodle dishes. Wakame, also called sea mustard, is a leafy green seaweed used in Japanese and Korean salads and soups. I think wakame, tossed with sesame seeds and a little sesame oil, makes a very flavorful salad. And if you've had miso soup, a staple in Japanese restaurants, that green leafy piece floating in the broth next to the tofu is wakame. Various types of kelp, like kombu, have been used throughout Asia, often dried and added to soups as flavoring. Sea grapes, raw but usually marinated in vinegar, are a common South Pacific salad ingredient. Dulse, another red algae (that actually is reddish-purple), is popular in Ireland, where it is cooked in vegetable dishes and soups. It's also dried and served as a salty snack food. And then there is saltwort, which grows in saltwater marshes.

At Sarasota's Mote Marine Laboratories, in their aquaculture division, marine biologists have been experimenting with waste by-product from red drum (redfish) to convert to fertilizer. Yes, you read that right. They're turning fish poop into fertilizer, and they're having considerable success using it for aquaponically grown saltwort and also for sea purslane, a shoreline plant. Both are catching on at some of Florida restaurants and markets.

caper butter sauce that was outstanding, as were my black-eyed peas and collard greens sides. Tripletail has a flavorful white meat similar to grouper. Its large rear upper and lower fins match up with the tail, hence the name. Other regular plates include pecan-crusted trout with crawfish butter; seared sea scallops with braised pork, succotash, and grits; jambalaya; shrimp-and-grits and sausage; and cornmeal-dusted catfish.

When you first walk up to Owen's Fish Camp's front porch, you'll see an old guy in an undershirt, with a fishing cap, sitting in a lawn chair and holding a can of beer. And he doesn't budge. That's because he's sculpture. My waitress told me it's Tate, the chef's granddad.

Walt's Fish Market and Restaurant, 4144 South Tamiami Trail, Sarasota 34231; (941) 921-4605; waltsfishmarketrestaurant.com. Walter "Walt" Wallin Sr. learned the commercial fishing business from his father, Claus, and his uncle Jessie Gallagher. Walt had just started a fish market business when World War II broke out and he joined the military. Upon returning he moved his family to Indiana for a while but then returned to Sarasota and opened Walt's Fish Market. It has remained a family business ever since. Walt's grandson Brett runs it now. With their own boats supplying the market and the restaurant, everything they offer today was likely swimming in the Gulf yesterday. The restaurant and the market share the same space. Order at the counter and they'll bring it to your table. The sandwich choices are extensive: not just grouper but also hog snapper, mangrove snapper, red snapper, cobia, soft-shell crab, and flounder. And there's shrimp prepared a variety of ways. Their shrimp salad is creamy and flavorful, and their peel-and-eat shrimp with Old Bay and garlic butter are some of the best I've tasted.

Siesta Key

The Lobster Pot, 5157 Ocean Boulevard, Siesta Key 34242; (941) 349-2323; sarasotalobsterpot.com. Glen and Kathy Medeiros, along with sons Tony and Mark, opened the Lobster Pot in 2001. Glen's father Ralph Medeiros, opened the family's original Lobster Pot in Cape Cod, Massachusetts, in 1940. To follow in his footsteps, Glen attended the Culinary Institute of America in New Haven, Connecticut, eventually ending up in the little beach town of Siesta Key, south of Sarasota. Most of the Lobster Pot's fresh fish comes from Florida waters, but the lobsters are flown in live from Maine. I came for lunch and enjoyed their New England Lobster Roll made with a quarter pound of fresh Maine lobster.

South Pasadena

Ted Peters Famous Smoked Fish, 1350 Pasadena Avenue South, South Pasadena 33707; (727) 381-3971; tedpetersfish.com. Some 70 years before roadside food trucks and trailers became all the rage, a guy named Ted Peters was serving smoked mullet out of a smoker on wheels set out in front of his restaurant on Blind Pass Road, between St. Pete Beach and Treasure Island. Peters had previously worked at the fisherman's co-op on nearby Madeira Beach (where he learned the smoking technique) before opening his small restaurant called the Blue Anchor. The smoker was essentially his roadside olfactory advertisement. In 1951 he moved the operation across the bridge to the St. Petersburg neighborhood of Pasadena, where it still is today. The smoked fish became his mainstay, and that merited the restaurant's name change. For a long time they only offered smoked mullet and on occasion, when it was available, Spanish mackerel. Now they offer salmon and mahi as well. Mullet sometimes gets a bad rap as too oily or chewy, but I find it just the opposite: light, flaky, and tender. At least it is when it comes from Ted Peters. Plus mullet seems to accept the smoking process very well, taking on that wonderful flavor

Seafood Lover's Florida

Eating Smoked Mullet

There are plenty of reasons not to eat smoked mullet. They are a lot of work to consume. They are full of bones. And you're going to smell like smoke for the rest of the day. There is one really good reason *to* eat smoked mullet though: It is some of the tastiest fish you will ever put in your mouth. Smoked mullet is not for everybody. But if you're willing to do the work, the reward is great. Mullet has a lot of bones, so it's a lot of work to eat. First grab the tail and gently pull it across the meat. That removes the backbone and most of the rib bones all at once. But there are still a lot of bones left in there. Gently "comb" the meat with your fork, in the direction that the bones point, and the tender, moist (if smoked properly) meat should come free. You are still going to end up getting some bones. Don't try to chew them up and swallow them. Just resign yourself to the fact that you will be spitting them out into a paper towel. Your fellow smoked-mullet diners will understand.

without being overpowered. Ted Peters smokes their fish over Florida red oak for about 6 hours, and it comes out perfectly moist and tasty. The other item that brings me here is Ted Peters outstanding homemade German potato salad.

St. Pete Beach

The Brass Monkey, 709 Gulf Way, Pass-a-Grille, St. Pete Beach 33706; (727) 367-7620; thebrassmonkey.net. The Brass Monkey is an outstanding seafood joint disguised as a sports bar. Well, actually they are a sports bar too. Their menu features some succulent selections, like grouper Annapolis stuffed with lump crab Imperial, and Atlantic salmon broiled with lemon-pepper seasoning. All excellent choices, but I always have to get the same thing when I come to the Brass Monkey: the broiled Maryland-style jumbo lump crab cakes. Owners Barry and Kelly Streib came to Pass-a-Grille from Maryland, where they ran a seafood restaurant for almost 2 decades, so they know crab.

Sea Critters, Pass-a-Grille, 2007 Pass-a-Grille Way, St. Pete Beach 33706; (727) 360-3706; seacritterscafe.com. Sea Critters overlooks the Intracoastal Waterway next to the Vina del Mar Bridge in Pass-a-Grille at the far-south end of St. Pete Beach. Patrons often arrive by boat. Some notable entrees include lobster pasta with spinach and tomatoes in a white wine sauce over angel-hair pasta; and a spicy jambalaya with andouille sausage and shrimp. But the best reason to come here is the fresh catch specials, always something a bit different than you find elsewhere. I had a superb triggerfish simply prepared: char-grilled with a key lime–butter sauce, and it was melt-in-your-mouth delicious.

Woody's Waterfront Cafe and Beach Bar, 308 Sunset Way, St. Pete Beach 33706; (727) 360-9165; woodyswaterfront.com. Woody's was just a bait house when it was built on Blind Pass Inlet in 1945, but by the 1950s it had evolved into a beer-and-burger joint. It hasn't changed much in the last 6 decades except now it's more of a beer-and-seafood joint. Fish sandwiches: Mahi, grouper, and sometimes snapper are popular items. I also like their skewered barbecued shrimp dinner.

St. Petersburg

The Casual Clam, 3336 9th Street North, St. Petersburg 33704;
(727) 895-2526; casualclam.com. My longtime mailman and good
friend Kerry Bolio (who grew up outside Boston, then lived 20 years in
Cape Cod, Massachusetts, and knows good seafood) told me about this
little neighborhood open-air bar-and-grill in St. Petersburg, with great
homemade clam chowder. "Go to Casual Clam and get a bowl of chowder
and a basket of fried belly clams," Kerry recommended, and I did. Belly
clams are whole clams, not just the strips of white meat (not to get too
graphic, but "belly" includes the intestines. I find them tastier, more like
oysters, and I love oysters!). Kerry was right. Casual Clam's clam chowder
is chock full of clams and vegetables. Casual Clam's bodacious belly
clams are flown in fresh from Ipswich, Massachusetts. New Englander
Paul Zareas opened Casual Clam in 1993. Today's owner, Larry Jackson,
took over in 1999 and continues Casual Clam's tradition of serving great,

Florida's Prehistoric Seafood Lovers

Weedon Island Preserve Cultural and Natural History Center 1800 Weedon Drive North East, St. Petersburg 33702; (727) 453-6500; weedonislandpreserve.org

Florida's first people likely arrived about 12,000 years ago. Back then its western coastline extended out 60 to 100 miles into what is now part of the Gulf of Mexico. There is plenty of evidence that Florida's aboriginals, primarily coastal dwellers, were highly dependent on fish and shellfish for their survival. The first Europeans arrived in the 15th century, and within 300 years all of Florida's original inhabitants were gone, mostly wiped out by diseases brought over by the Europeans for which the Florida aboriginals had no developed immunities.

Career geologist David Burns (master's degree in geology) became interested in archaeology in the early 1990s and began pursuing it in earnest when he started working with the Central Gulf Coast Archaeological Society in Florida. In 2001 he was invited to work at Weedon Island on Tampa Bay in St. Petersburg, where the new Weedon Island Cultural Center was going to be built. The center opened in 2002, but the first Weedon Island excavations began in 1923 under the auspices of Dr. Jesse Walter Fewkes, director of the Bureau of Ethnology at the Smithsonian Institute.

I got to sit down with David Burns and learn about some of Florida's earliest seafood gatherers and consumers. David explained, "The Weedon Island culture is known for its high-quality pottery. Pottery is the main thing archaeologists use in Florida to identify time frames and cultures. A lot of it is based on design. For instance, the earlier pottery had fiber, like Spanish moss, mixed in the clay."

It seems we can get the best picture of how these people lived by rummaging through their trash: digging in mounds called "trash middens."

"When we excavate we usually find shells: oysters, scallops, clams, and whelks," David told me. "They made good use of whatever they had. They couldn't exactly run down to the nearest Publix or Home Depot, so they had to be pretty inventive. They would use clam shells for bowls and whelk shells for spoons or ladles. We find turtle bones, deer bones, snake bones. The middens, their trash mounds, is where we get the best idea of how they ate, what they subsided on, what time of year they collected it and consumed it. Sometimes you'll see a layer of oysters and then maybe a layer of scallops, indicating what was most plentiful at a certain time. Of course, today we go to a restaurant and gladly pay big bucks for fresh oysters, but I can picture them back then saying, 'Oh, we're not having oysters *again*, are we?'"

Apparently they weren't much of an agrarian culture. There was no need for farming. "It was mostly gathering. Most everything was right there for them. All they had to do was collect it. They did apparently travel some, however, to collect things like squash and other gourd plants."

I asked David how they fished. "They had multiple ways. Sometimes we'll find what look like hooks made out of bone— like carved deer bone. Another type of hook that they made was like a bone hairpin, tapered at both ends and tied in the middle. They would put bait on it, and when the fish would hit it, the tapered ends would hang in the fish's mouth. Sometimes they would spear fish. Another way they fished was with netting. They also had baskets with an open end where they could funnel the fish when the tide was going out. They were pretty ingenious and seemed to be adept at making use of their environment."

Who were they? "We call them Tocobagans, but of course we don't know what they called themselves. They covered the Tampa Bay area, around Pinellas and Hillsborough Counties, but not too far south. There was the Manasota culture down in the Sarasota area (earlier than the Tocobagan). If you went farther south, there was the Calusa. They all seemed to have their defined territories. The Tocobagans were here in this Weedon Island area from about AD 200 to AD 900. There was contact and commerce between groups and a surprising amount of trade. We find shells up in the Carolinas, Alabama, and Georgia. And we find copper and a lot of flint and other stones from up north down here. The rivers were like their freeways, and that gave them easy access using their long, log canoes."   (continued)

What did they prefer to eat? "We find the shells and broken pottery but rarely find any remains [of the actual food]. We can collect what's called a column sample, and do a flotation, where we soak it in water so that seeds and other stuff will float up to the top. Then we can get some idea of the vegetation they ate. For shellfish, we find a lot of oyster, some scallops, some clams, mussels, and whelks. They also ate a lot of mullet, some sea trout, and catfish. And they also drank what we call the 'Black Drink,' made from dried leaves from the cassina bush. It was kind of like their espresso."

How did they prepare their food? "They would build a fire and cook directly in it or smoke fish over it on racks. Mostly they put big pots close to or in a fire, filled it with whatever they had collected—oysters, clams, sea grapes—and let it stew all day. We know that because of the soot we find on the outside of pots. They also used the pots for storing and transporting food."

David and other archaeologists at Weedon Island continue to unearth the remains of this slice of early Florida civilization and learn more about how the Tocobagans lived. One project they are working on currently is carefully excavating a 40-foot-long canoe found here that may actually predate the Tocobagans. The excavation should be complete and the canoe should be on display at Weedon Island Preserve Cultural and Natural History Center by the time this book goes to print.

One thing I find remarkable is how much of these original inhabitants' seafood preparation and eating habits still survive today. A big pot of oysters, clams, scallops, and sea grapes, stewing all day over a fire, sounds an awful lot like a Low Country Boil. And cooking on and smoking over an open fire is not much different than backyard barbecuing today. I'm also impressed with their inventiveness. Shells were cleverly fashioned into eating utensils and cooking tools, and fish bones were turned into fish hooks. And their basket nets that captured fish by funneling them during outgoing tides are very similar in function to the trawling nets modern shrimpers use today.

fresh seafood. And it's not just clams. They also have fried or peel-and-eat shrimp, scallops, crab cakes, and a Fried Fisherman's Platter with shrimp, oysters, scallops, haddock, and of course whole belly clams.

Crab Shack Restaurant, 11400 Gandy Boulevard, St. Petersburg 33702; (727) 576-7813; crabshack.com. There is no shortage of Tampa Bay–area restaurants offering good grouper sandwiches. Frenchy's in Clearwater Beach started the trend, and now it is the staple of every Florida seafood restaurant. They come fried, grilled, Cajun-style, jerked, buffalo-style, even Reuben-style with Swiss cheese and sauerkraut, but my preference is blackened: not just sprinkled with blackening seasoning but genuinely seared black in a cast-iron skillet. The original "blackened" fish was redfish, and New Orleans chef Paul Prudhomme mixed his own Black Magic seasoning, which he caked liberally on a redfish fillet, then dropped it in a scalding cast-iron skillet with butter and seared it black on both sides. It is difficult to find anyone who does it that way anymore, but Tyrone Dayhoff, manager of the Crab Shack Restaurant, does. The

Crab Shack's cast-iron skillet sits on the stove, on high heat, all day, and they use Paul Prudhomme's Black Magic seasoning. For the longest time they did it with grouper, but in the first decade of the 21st century when grouper became scarce, Dayhoff began looking for a suitable alternative that would work as well with cast-iron-skillet blackening. He tried Atlantic cod and discovered that it tasted as good as (maybe even better than?) grouper, and the Blackened Super Shack Fish Sandwich has been cod ever since.

The flotsam-and-jetsam-decorated Crab Shack has anchored the west side of Gandy Bridge in St. Petersburg for 7 decades. It was originally called the Illinois Inn when it opened in 1947. They are actually best known for their blue-crab claws, either fried or sautéed in butter and garlic. And there's more crab: blue-crab cakes, stone crab claws, and soft-shell crab, in addition to fresh-shucked oysters, peel-and-eat shrimp, yellowfin tuna, snapper, catfish, and smoked mullet.

Fourth Street Shrimp Store Restaurant, 1006 4th Street North, St. Petersburg 33701; (727) 822-0325; theshrimpstore.com. Owner Brian Connell opened Fourth Street Shrimp Store in 1984 in what had originally been a 1928 garage and service station. In 1997 he expanded out front, adding the current bar, dining area, and front porch. Casual atmosphere, kitschy decorations, and good, simple fresh-catch seafood are what this place is about. Obviously shrimp is the main menu item: with fried, steamed U-Peel-'Em, scampi, and shrimp pasta—Alfredo or marinara— offered as dinners. There's also lobster-and-shrimp salad, shrimp po'boys, shrimp cocktails, and shrimp tacos, which I had. Mine came grilled, with creamy remoulade sauce and mango salsa, and hit the spot. They also have mahimahi, ahi tuna steak, grouper, basa, salmon, cod, and catfish dinners, plus salmon or ahi tuna Veracruz, with sautéed onions, mushrooms, peppers, and tomatoes.

I. C. Sharks, 13040 Gandy Boulevard, St. Petersburg 33702; (727) 498-8568; icsharks.com. A relative newcomer, about a block from the Crab Shack, I. C. Sharks has both a seafood market and an alfresco tiki-hut cafe out back that backs up to a small inlet off Tampa Bay. Their raw bar offerings include a tasty tuna tartare with some kick—marinated in citrus, soy, wasabi, jalapeños, and sriracha; and their steamed peel-and-eat shrimp are plump and dusted with cayenne seasoning for a little hotter flavor.

Locale Market, 179 2nd Avenue North, St. Petersburg 33701, (727) 523-6300; localegourmetmarket.com. Downtown St. Petersburg's BayWalk shopping, restaurant, and movie complex had been slipping for a couple years when St. Petersburg developer Bill Edwards bought it in 2011. In 2012 and 2013 he closed it all up and remodeled the entire city block into Sundial St. Pete, which opened in 2014. One of Sundial's centerpieces is the Locale Market, a gourmet food marketplace owned by chefs Michael Mina and Don Pintabona. Locale features separate stations for different types

of food, with an emphasis on very fresh, seasonal, and of course "local": fruits and vegetables (including seaweed; see the sidebar "Seafood for Vegans?" on p. 99) at one stand, Italian food at another, and a butcher shop with dry aged beef, sausages, bacon, pork, and even rabbit. But I'm most intrigued by the seafood station, which occupies the center of the market. They offer fresh Gulf whole and filleted fish including swordfish, snapper, and grouper, plus all types of shellfish—oysters, clams, mussels, shrimp, and lobster. And they also prepare some marvelous walk-away seafood dishes like salmon poke, consisting of cubed raw salmon in a sweet honey-sesame-soy sauce, and grilled octopus salad with chickpeas and tomatoes.

The Oyster Bar, 249 Central Avenue, St. Petersburg 33701; (727) 897-9728; theoysterbarstpete.com. As you move inland a couple blocks from Downtown St. Petersburg's waterfront, Central Avenue becomes the center of activity. Among the bars and shops is a place that used to be called Central Avenue Oyster Bar, now simply the Oyster Bar. They will shuck raw oysters for you at the bar for as long as you'll eat them, or you can have their version of Rockefeller with spinach and a little chorizo sausage, or Kilpatrick with bacon and barbecue sauce, or blue cheese topped. Noteworthy among the selection of seafood entrees are crawfish

pasta, grilled cobia with pineapple salsa and avocado puree, and bacon-Parmesan-crusted red grouper.

Red Mesa, 4912 4th Street North, St. Petersburg 33703; (727) 527-8728; redmesarestaurant.com. Who would ever expect a Mexican restaurant to be one of the best seafood restaurants in the Tampa Bay area? But Red Mesa in St. Petersburg defies so many of our preconceived notions of what a Mexican restaurant is.

Red Mesa executive chef Chris Fernandez's apprenticeship began when he was 5 years old. He grew up in Oaxaca, in south Mexico, where his family owned two restaurants. In 1994 Fernandez, who had worked at the St. Petersburg Pier location of Columbia Restaurant and then at the Vinoy Hotel, began working part-time for Peter and Shawn Veytia at their popular 4th Street seafood restaurant, the Seabar. Before long the Veytia's began letting Fernandez create some of his own specials. In 1996 they decided it was time to give the Seabar a rebirth into a Mexican and Southwestern restaurant. Peter's background is Cuban, Shawn's is Mexican, as is Chris's, so Latin seemed a natural direction to take.

Red Mesa's menu features delectable authentic regional Mexican, as well as Caribbean, Cuban, and Spanish dishes. Start with one of the three kinds of ceviche: conch, grouper, or shrimp aguachile, or maybe a crab-and-shrimp empanada. For an entree consider the Grouper Al Mojo De Ajo, with garlic, tomatoes, parsley, and *chile de arbol*; the Chipotle Shrimp, cooked in chipotle chile butter, with *queso fresco* (Mexican fresh goat cheese) and cilantro on a corn tortilla; or either the Cedar-Roasted or Ginger-Crusted Salmon.

When I met and interviewed Chris Fernandez for a *DuPont Registry* magazine article a few years back he gave me the recipe for his Camarones al Jerez: shrimp in sherry, olive oil, and garlic. He told me it was designed to be relatively easy to make, and it is. I've made it many times. See it in the "In the Kitchen" section in the back of the book.

Sea Salt, 183 2nd Avenue North, St. Petersburg 33701; (727) 873-7964; seasaltstpete.com. Sundial St. Pete's anchor upscale restaurant is Sea Salt. The decor is elegant and minimalist in a midcentury modern kind of way, and their towering glass 2-story-tall wine cellar makes an impressive centerpiece. Venice, Italy–born owner and chef Fabrizio Aielli has given his restaurant a theme that fits with his seaside-Italy upbringing. As the name suggests, that theme is various flavorings of salt. All dinners start with

bread and olive oil and several regional choices of salt for dipping. When I was here we had Hawaiian, Himalayan, and Indian (that tasted distinctly like hard-boiled egg). Sea Salt's entrees are elegant and minimalist in preparation. If you like, you can pick out your fresh fish from their cooler. I had the grilled swordfish, cooked perfectly, with a lemon-butter sauce and polenta as the side. A couple other interesting entrees: pistachio-parsley-crusted ahi tuna and barbecued Ora King Salmon.

Tampa

Big Ray's Fish Camp, 6116 Interbay Boulevard, Tampa 33611; (813) 605-3615; bigraysfishcamp.com. For a long time the tiny concrete-block building on South Tampa's Interbay Boulevard was home to Chubasco Seafood Market, but in 2015 Nick Cruz bought it and began turning it into Big Ray's Fish Camp restaurant. Nick's first name is actually Raymond— "Big Ray" refers to his grandfather. Nick comes from a family long entrenched in both fishing and cooking. Many of the old black-and-white photos on the wall are of his grandfather. Inside there are just 4 tables, plus a counter with some stools, but outside they have picnic tables, and soon, they tell me, they will be expanding onto the property next door. Their motto, "From our bay to your belly," reminds patrons that Big Ray's is big on "fresh out of the water and into the frying pan." On my first visit I had their outstanding grilled grouper sandwich—one of the best I've had, but for all my return visits I have ordered their signature entree: the lobster corn dog. It's an entire lobster tail deep-fried in corn dog batter on a stick, and it is magnificent!

The Columbia Restaurant, several locations. 2117 East 7th Avenue, Ybor City, Tampa 33605; (813) 248-4961. 801 Old Water Street #1905, Tampa 33602; (813) 229-5511; columbiarestaurant.com. Additional locations in Celebration, Sarasota, St. Augustine, and at the Tampa airport. The Columbia is not just Florida's oldest Latin restaurant, it's Florida's oldest continuously operating restaurant, period. It is also the largest Spanish restaurant in the United States. Casimiro Hernandez opened the Columbia in Ybor City (east Tampa) in 1905. Like many Cubans at the turn of that century, Casimiro Hernandez came, in 1904, from Havana to Tampa, where the cigar business was beginning to flourish. But he was interested in food, not cigars, and in 1905 he opened a small cafe on the corner of 7th Avenue and 22nd Street in Tampa's Latin Ybor City. He named it "the Columbia" after "Columbia, the Gem of the Ocean," a patriotic song popular during the Civil War. It was a small cafe that served mostly 2 Spanish dishes: garbanzo bean soup and *arroz con pollo* (chicken and yellow rice), along with a sandwich that was invented in Ybor City, the Cuban sandwich. His cafe's popularity grew quickly, and before long Hernandez partnered with the La Fonda Restaurant next door and turned that into the Columbia's dining room. Casimiro passed away in 1929, and his oldest son, also named Casimiro, took over, right at the start of the Great Depression. In defiance of the failing economy, Casimiro II expanded the Columbia, adding additional rooms and bringing in live music in the evenings, and it worked. Today musicians still perform Spanish music for evening diners at the original Ybor City Columbia. Casimiro Jr.'s daughter, Adela Hernandez, a Juilliard-trained concert pianist, married Cesar Gonzmart, a concert violinist. For a while they traveled and performed around the country, but in 1953 Adela's father's health had begun to fail and they returned to run the Columbia. The rest

is restaurant history. Today Casimiro Hernandez's great-grandson Richard Gonzmart runs the Columbia empire, with seven Columbia Restaurants plus a new venue, Ulele (see below).

In the recipe section at the back of this book, you will find Columbia Restaurant's recipe for Grouper (or Merluza, Snapper, or Trout) a la Rusa. When I was growing up in Tampa, Trout a la Rusa (Trout Russian) was always one of my favorites, but somewhere along the way grouper's popularity overtook trout (considered a bit oily by some, but not me), and the Columbia now makes the dish with merluza, a white, flaky fish similar to cod. No matter. Same recipe, different fish. A merluza (or trout, or grouper, or snapper) fillet, lightly seasoned with garlic powder, is pan-fried in butter in a skillet and then covered with thin lemon slices, chopped hard-boiled egg, and parsley. This is the dish that introduced me to fish at a very young age. Another Spanish specialty that you will find at the Columbia is pompano papillote: pompano cooked in a paper bag with a spicy Tabasco-nutmeg cream sauce, along with layers of shrimp and lobster or crawfish. But the granddaddy of all Spanish seafood dishes is paella Valenciana: lobster, shrimp, oysters, mussels, scallops, blue crabs, and snapper, plus green and red peppers, tomatoes, onions, peas, garlic, saffron, and rice are all cooked into one giant marvelous dish, usually prepared for at least 4 people.

Green Iguana, 4029 South Westshore Boulevard, Tampa 33611; (813) 837-1234. 1708 East 7th Avenue, Ybor City/Tampa 33605; (813) 248-9555; greeniguana.com. When the Green Iguana opened on South Tampa's

Westshore Boulevard in 1995, there weren't very many local bar and grills that offered both good local entertainment and good food. That formula has been copied quite a bit since, but Green Iguana is still one of the best. In their early days they had a real live (and pretty big) pet iguana, Iggy, who lived up on the mantle behind the bar. These days I'm certain that would violate somebody's health code or food establishment ordinance, but back then Iggy was a much-loved celebrity. The food was good back then, and it's maybe even better now. Originally it was just burgers and grouper sandwiches, but today's menu has expanded, even moved a little upscale. Appetizers now include spicy garlic shrimp, tuna sashimi, and some of the best conch fritters I've found anywhere. For entrees they've added grouper piccata and a Taste of Key West: grilled mahi, salmon, or grouper, with coconut rice and mango salsa. And they still make one of the best grouper sandwiches in South Tampa.

Hula Bay, 5210 West Tyson Avenue, Tampa 33611; (813) 837-4852; hulabayclub.com. In 2009 Green Iguana's owners Rick Caldaroni and Amir Mahdieh and business partner Loren Rhoads bought a Tampa Bay waterfront restaurant called Rattlefish (it was at a location on the bay called Rattlesnake Point, and they served fish. I know, nobody else got it either.). Wisely the new owners gave it a new theme and name, Hawaiian and "Hula

Bay." They've applied their culinary skills honed at Green Iguana and taken it upscale another notch. Their menu includes a tangy ceviche martini appetizer with shrimp, scallops, and fish; black mussels in wine, garlic, and lemon butter sauce; and Kick'n Shrimp in a barbecue, garlic, and Kona beer sauce. One of my favorite main courses is their Lacquered Sesame Salmon coated in a sweet teriyaki sauce and served with bok choy. They also have terrific shrimp, mahi, and grouper tacos and an extensive sushi menu. One more thing: Hula Bay has the distinction of being the only Tampa-side bay-front restaurant with its own docks, accessible by boat.

Oystercatchers, 2900 Bayport Drive, Tampa 33607; (813) 207-6815; hyatt.com/gallery/oystercatchers. While Oystercatchers is part of the Grand Hyatt Tampa Bay Hotel, it has its own completely separate location at the south end of their 35-acre nature preserve property. Request a window seat and a reservation just before sunset, and you might see rabbits hopping among the mangroves along the shoreline of the bay. Oystercatchers has been one of Tampa's top restaurants for 4 decades, and seafood is their area of expertise. They buy whole fish fresh each morning, and you can pick out your own catch from their display case if you like. Among a wide assortment of starters and appetizers, I have to begin with a small bowl of the she-crab bisque and their shrimp-and-crab fritters with mango-lemon dipping sauce, or sometimes I'll opt for the Bay Scallop Ceviche. Main course specialties include a lobster mac-and-cheese made with goat cheese and gruyère, and a prosciutto-wrapped grouper saltimbocca, but I usually go for something out of the fresh-catch-of-the-day case, pecan-wood grilled. Oh yes, and their just-baked sourdough bread will convince you you're in San Francisco.

Rick's on the River, 2305 North Willow Avenue, Tampa 33607; (813) 251-0369; ricksontheriver.com. On the opposite bank of the Hillsborough River from Ulele and upriver a bit, you'll find Rick's on the River. With their own dock and marina, and large outdoor seating area, Rick's has been particularly popular with boaters since it opened in 1994. Seafood dominates the menu, and they're known for their fresh oysters: on the half shell or steamed with pepper-jack cheese or a basket of fried oysters. The oyster or shrimp po'boys are also popular, and I like Rick's Fish Sandwich, usually grouper and sometimes snapper. They offer it blackened, fried, jerk seasoned, or my preference, lemon-pepper grilled.

Skipper's Smokehouse, 910 Skipper Road, Tampa 33613; (813) 971-0666; skipperssmokehouse.com. The rambling weathered-wood-and-corrugated-tin structure that is Skipper's Smokehouse began as a much smaller biker beer-and-burger joint in 1977. Skipper wasn't the restaurant owner. John Skipper owned a large tract of land in this area a century ago. The road is named for him, and the restaurant is named after the road. In 1980 Air Force veteran Tom White bought Skipper's with help from a couple of his Air Force buddies. It was Tom and his friends who built the Skipper's we know and love today. Since Skipper's has always been known as a venue for live blues, zydeco, and rock 'n' roll, the food has always taken

a backseat. Yes, John Lee Hooker has played here, and every Thursday night the house band, Uncle John's Band, plays Grateful Dead favorites, but do not discount the food. Oysters, raw or steamed, top their list of specialties, with smoked mullet a close second. They also do great beer-boiled peel-and-eat shrimp, broiled catfish, and a heaping Skipper's Platter with fried shrimp, oysters, basa (a type of catfish), gator tail, and a side of their smoked fish dip.

Taste of Boston, 5314 Interbay Boulevard, Tampa 33611; (813) 831-2112; tasteofbostonsouthtampa.com. Imagine this: You can get some of South Tampa's freshest seafood at the very spot where science-fiction novelist Jules Verne imagined a moon rocket launch. In his 1865 novel *From the Earth to the Moon*, three astronauts launch from "Stone's Hill" in "Tampa Town, Florida." Although in the book he miscalculated the longitude and latitude (his numbers are actually closer to Port Charlotte), the spot that Verne identifies is called Ballast Point. His selection was prescient. Nearly a hundred years later, NASA would choose Cape Canaveral, directly across the state, for that same purpose. The "ballast" in Ballast Point refers to ship ballast stones dumped at the mouth of Old Tampa Bay. The stones that litter the bottom here have long been an attraction for fish and crabs, making this a popular fishing spot.

Taste of Boston overlooks the park's fishing pier, lending a maritime ambience to the restaurant. This is a no-frills, plastic-forks-and-knives kind of place, and the service can be haphazard at times. But the seafood is always very fresh. Preparation is simple but consistently good. The original owners were northeasterners, and Taste of Boston's creamy, chunky clam chowder is one of their specialties. Be forewarned: If you sit outside for that waterfront ambience, you may find a seagull or two competing for your meal.

Ulele, 1810 North Highland Avenue, Tampa 33602; (813) 999-4952; ulele .com. Ulele, which opened in August 2014, is one of Columbia Restaurant (see above) owner Richard Gonzmart's most ambitious projects. More than just a restaurant, this was also a complex historic building restoration, and it was key to the revitalization of downtown Tampa's riverfront Tampa Heights district.

First, the building: This was Tampa's Water Works Building, built in 1903. And the location. Ulele now anchors the north end of Tampa's River- walk, a park that follows the east bank of the Hillsborough River from the

What Is a Deviled Crab and Where Are the Best Places to Get One?

I first began eating lunch at La Tropicana Cafe on 7th Avenue in Ybor City in 1973. I was in high school and working part-time in the family's truck sales business driving a parts delivery truck. One of our truck salesmen, Braxton Harrell, would ask me to stop off at La Tropicana, if my deliveries took me through the neighborhood near lunchtime, to pick up some deviled crabs (he called them belly bombs). I immediately became hooked on them, and before long I was

south end of downtown, up to the new Water Works Park. And the name: Ulele is the name of a legendary Tocobagan native Floridian princess who, in 1528, pleaded with her father, the chief, to save the life of captured Spanish sailor Juan Ortiz (before they might roast him alive), who was on an expedition searching for missing explorer Panfilo de Narvaez. By the way, this happened 100 years before Pocahontas saved the life of John Smith.

making sure my delivery route took me by La Tropicana at least three or four times a week.

In case anyone thinks that a deviled crab is simply crabmeat wrapped in dough and deep-fried, read this list of ingredients (from a Columbia Restaurant recipe, courtesy of *The Gasparilla Cookbook*). The dough: stale American bread (soaked and then squeezed dry), stale Cuban bread (ground fine and sifted), all mixed with paprika and salt and then refrigerated for a couple hours. The crab filling: onions, green bell pepper, cloves of garlic, crushed red hot pepper, bay leaves, sugar, salt, tomato paste, and of course fresh blue-crab claw meat. According to *Cigar City* magazine (an Ybor City history publication), Tampa's first deviled crabs were sold in the early 1920s from a street cart in Ybor City by Tampa native Francisco Oscar Miranda. He was known to everyone as the Deviled Crab Man. Miranda made his deviled crabs daily, with essentially the same ingredients listed above, and sold them from his cart for 3 decades until his passing in 1953. So what's the "deviled" part about? It's about heat. Traditionally deviled crabs are split and doused with hot sauce, plus they already have hot red pepper flakes in the crab filling mixture.

Here are four places to get great deviled crabs in Tampa:

La Tropicana Cafe 1822 East 7th Avenue, Ybor City, Tampa 33605; (813) 247-4040

Brocato's Sandwich Shop 5021 East Columbus Drive, Tampa 33619; (813) 248-9977; brocatossandwich.com

Aguila Sandwich Shop 3200 West Hillsborough Avenue, Tampa 33614; (813) 876-4022

The Columbia Restaurant 2117 East 7th Avenue, Ybor City, Tampa 33605; (813) 248-4961; columbiarestaurant.com

Now for the food: Gonzmart's appreciation for native-to-Florida shines through here, so seafood features prominently. For an adventurous beginning, try the alligator hush puppies, with gator meat, ham, duck bacon, corn, and jalapeño. Many of the dishes are cooked on their 10-foot-diameter *barbacoa* open grill. A staple in the Tocobagan diet was oysters, and Ulele offers them 4 different ways: raw on the half shell, Oyster Cabbage Boats in kale and apple cabbage cups, Patron in sangria and tequila, and my favorite, charbroiled over the *barbacoa* grill with garlic, butter, and Parmesan and Romano cheeses. For main courses, in addition to a daily-changing fresh-catch list, try Juan's (presumably in honor of the almost-roasted Juan Ortiz?) Horno (Oven)-Roasted Snapper Fillet, or their Deconstructed Seafood Pot Pie with grouper, shrimp, roasted oysters, and an assortment of vegetables in a wine cream sauce, pastry on the side.

Tarpon Springs

Paul's, 530 Athens Street, Tarpon Springs 34689; (727) 938-5093; paulsshrimp.com. Back in the 1980s Paul's was the place where my buddies and I would go for Greek Peperi Garethes—peppered peel-and-eat shrimp—and beer. It was mostly just a bar with long tables where we could all feast on giant buckets of steamed shrimp, but it dated back to the 1940s, and it was a place where you would likely share a table with a Greek fisherman. It was a neighborhood joint and it had a history. But then they closed. They reopened in a new location, but somehow it just wasn't the same. Eventually that location closed too. But recently Paul's opened up once again, in their old original Athens Street spot. You can get great peel-and-eat shrimp in a bunch of different places now, but there is something nostalgic about Paul's for me.

Rusty Bellie's Waterfront Grill and Pelican Point Seafood Market, 937 Dodecanese Boulevard, Tarpon Springs 34689; (727) 934-4047; rustybellies.com. Julie Reis Russell's family came to Tarpon Springs and got into the commercial fishing and shrimping business in the 1970s. Her parents opened J. Reis Seafood (now Pelican Point Seafood Market) in 1979 at the west end of Dodecanese Boulevard in the Tarpon Springs sponge docks district. Julie and her husband, Jack Russell, took over the business in 1985, and then in 2005 they opened Rusty Bellie's Grill next door to Pelican Point Seafood. By the way, a "rusty bellie," they say, is a big gag grouper. Their menu is a veritable cornucopia of fresh-off-the-boat seafood items like mahimahi, mullet, and grouper, including a Greek-style version called the Kay Lyn, topped with onions, peppers, sun-dried tomatoes, and feta cheese in a garlic tomato sauce. In addition, they offer a succulent selection of steamed clams, stone crab claws, and my favorite, peel-and-eat shrimp in lemon and olive oil, although this time I went for

Sponge Capital of the World

When the first Greek sponge divers came to Tarpon Springs over a century ago, no one could have envisioned the cultural transformation that their arrival would bring. Today the community is wholly identified by its rich Greek heritage and traditions.

Philadelphia investor John Cheyney began buying Tarpon Springs property in 1887. One of his side ventures was the Anclote and Rock Island Sponge Company. At the time, sponges were harvested from boats using long poles with hooks. But that changed when John hired a young Greek immigrant named John Corcoris, who suggested a better way to collect the sponges. In Corcoris's family home of Hydra, Greece, divers harvested sponges wearing heavy copper helmets and canvas-and-rubber suits, with air pumped through tubes from a boat on the surface. With financial backing from Cheyney, Corcoris persuaded sponge divers from the Greek islands, including his brothers, to come to Tarpon Springs. In 1905 the Corcoris brothers outfitted their first sponge-diving boat. By the end of that summer, 500 Greek sponge divers had come to Tarpon Springs from the islands of Hydra and Aegena, south of Athens; and Kalymnos, Symi, and Halki, in the Dodecanese Islands. Two years after that the Sponge Exchange, an auction house and storage-and-grading facility, opened, and before long Tarpon Springs had gained its reputation as the Sponge Capital of the World.

By the 1970s tourism had begun to surpass sponge harvesting as Tarpon Springs's largest industry, but along the way other businesses grew as a result of the Greek immigration, notably, boat construction and Greek restaurants. Today Tarpon Springs is perhaps as well known for its extraordinary food as it is for its sponge-diving history.

the grilled shrimp. If you can't decide which to try, get the Rusty's Pot Belly with steamed shrimp, oysters, clams, mussels, snow crab, and corn and potatoes, all in one bowl.

Tierra Verde

Billy's Stone Crab and Seafood Restaurant, 1 Collany Road, Tierra Verde 33715; (727) 866-2115; billysstonecrab.com. Tierra Verde resident and property developer Billy Moore opened Billy's Stone Crab overlooking Hurricane Hole Inlet in 1981, but his experience in seafood restaurants goes back to 1972, when he opened Billy's Moorings on Corey Avenue in St. Pete Beach. Billy's Stone Crab has an extensive selection of seafood items on their menu, like wild-caught mahi with mango salsa, and plump grilled deep-sea scallops. Some diners even come for the steaks (they have a reputation for having the best steaks of any seafood restaurant in the

Stone Crab Claws: Collecting and Cracking

First, let me point out that stone-crab-claw harvesting is unique in the crab-collecting world. The crab survives. Stone crab fishermen take only the single larger claw, and return the live crab to the sea where they will grow a new claw.

As for cracking stone crab claws, everybody seems to have their own "definitive" way to go about it, and I am no exception. Most use some type of hinged cracker or a mallet, but I find that both risk smashing some of the meat along with the shell. My technique uses a large metal stirring spoon in the right hand and the stone crab claw cupped in the left hand. The cupping is important because it distributes the shock of the whack throughout the claw, thereby minimizing the impact on one spot. The spoon is turned around backwards so that you are whacking with the rounded part. The trick is to not hit too hard, just "flick" the claw (and knuckles) with several moderate hits until a few cracks spider-web across one another. Then stop. You're done. Pull the cracked shell pieces off the meat and enjoy.

Tampa Bay area). But most come to Billy's for the stone crab claws, which they get fresh off the boat direct from a select group of Gulf Coast crabbers that Billy's has worked with for decades. Get the largest size they offer that day: Jumbos or Colossals are best. Less cracking, more eating.

Treasure Island

Middle Grounds Grill, 10925 Gulf Boulevard, Treasure Island 33706; (727) 360-4253; middlegroundsgrill.com. When Treasure Island restaurateur Dave Coover decided in 2005 to remodel what was a pancake house into an upscale seafood restaurant, he picked a name that would tie it to seafood in a locally recognizable way. The Gulf of Mexico's "Middle Grounds" is a vast (over 450 square miles) mid-shelf bank about 100 miles offshore, west-northwest of St. Pete Beach. Ample corals and rock bottom make this home to an abundance of sea life like amberjack, snapper, hogfish, and of course grouper. Both commercial and recreational fishermen have fished this region for eons. So it is no surprise that at Middle Grounds Grill, grouper features prominently: grilled, fried, blackened, or sautéed, or pistachio-and-macadamia-nut-crusted with a mango beurre blanc sauce. Their honey-ginger-glazed salmon is another tempting option. For appetizers try the fried calamari with ginger sauce or the lemon-infused crab cakes.

Weeki Wachee

Becky Jack's Food Shack, 8070 Cortez Boulevard, Weeki Wachee 34607; (352) 610-4412; beckyjacks.com. After spending a day kayaking the Weeki Wachee River with my niece, the intrepid Dr. Cameron McNabb, we were famished and looking for good local grub. Cameron jumped on her smartphone and immediately came up with Becky Jack's Food Shack, right down the road, and what a great find.

Becky De La Rosa opened the Food Shack (it was just Becky's then) back in the 1970s. Then in 2009 Kimberlee Curtis and her husband, Joe Foster, bought it and put "Jack" in the name, an homage to their friend and restaurant mentor Jack Newkirk, who owned Newk's Sports Bar in Tampa. Becky Jack's is a tiny place, but it's filled to the brim with character (and with characters). There's a 1960s theme going on here, with wait staff  clad in tie-dyed psychedelic T-shirts and a background soundtrack by the Doors, Herman's Hermits, and the Beatles. The menu features a variety of fish sandwiches. The fish can vary with whatever they get fresh that day, but they serve it grilled, blackened, or "crunchy," which means fried in their proprietary Corn Flake and almond batter. They also make it as a Reuben. I've had the fish tacos, the Crunchy Fish Sandwich, and last time in I had the blackened mahi sandwich, which was outstanding. There is sad news: Kimberlee passed away in 2015. But Becky Jack's was as busy as always on my most recent visit and Kimberlee's exuberance and spirit definitely still permeate the place.

Central East

Throughout the first half of the 20th century, central-east Florida was mostly drive-across country. Orlando was a sleepy, medium-size town whose existence depended primarily on citrus farming. But that all changed in 1965.

Popular legend about how Walt Disney secretly bought up citrus groves and swampland in Central Florida is largely true. As early as 1963, Walt and his brother Roy began searching for a Florida location for a second park: Disney World. Disneyland, which had opened in Anaheim, California, in 1955, dismayed Disney. He had purposely built it in a high-population area but never anticipated the garish impact his park would make on the city surrounding it. Walt vowed that, at his next theme park, he would do it differently.

Vast and inexpensive acreage near good highways was available just west of Orlando. Walt and Roy went to extreme lengths to keep the land purchases under wraps, buying a patch-quilt of small plots, 5 to 10 acres at a time, usually for less than $200 per acre. They used dummy corporations with names like Retlaw (Walter spelled backwards) Enterprises and Latin American Development Corporation. Although Walt Disney flew over the area numerous times, he never once set foot out of the airplane for fear of being recognized. When word that Disney was buying finally leaked out in a 1965 *Orlando Sentinel* story, prices shot to $80,000 per acre. Today I-4 is known almost as much for its legendary traffic jams as it is for being the road that leads to Disney World (and a plethora of additional theme parks). But that growth has also attracted the attention of some legendary restaurateurs and chefs, including one Florida's best: Norman Van Aken, owner of Norman's at the Ritz-Carlton.

Florida's central-east coast saw big changes as well in the 1960s. After Bill France completed his 2½-mile high-banked Daytona International Speedway in 1959, the town of Daytona Beach was transformed forever. But perhaps the biggest change came in 1961 when NASA's Project Mercury put its first astronaut, Alan Shepard, into space. Although the Air Force had been testing rocket launches at Cape Canaveral since 1950, it was the Mercury, Gemini, and Apollo programs of the 1960s and the development of Kennedy Space Center that generated enormous growth along the coast here. There are, however, still stretches of this coast that are lightly populated and largely undeveloped, particularly just north of Cape Canaveral. And I found two of my favorite seafood shacks here: Goodrich Seafood Restaurant in Oak Hill on the east side of the Mosquito Lagoon, and JB's Fish Camp on its west side just south of New Smyrna Beach.

•••———————•••••———————•••

Astor

Blackwater Inn, 55716 Front Street, Astor 32102; (352) 759-2802; blackwaterinn.com. Good friend and author of *Umatilla, A Photographic History* (Arcadia Publishing 2010) Becky Dreisbach was working on an article about the Ocala National Forest for my *Car and Diner* blog when she took me to the Blackwater Inn, on the west bank of the St. Johns River

in Astor. It opened in 1974 here alongside the State Road 40 Bridge, overlooking a picturesque stretch of the St. Johns. Their menu includes some Florida Cracker specialties like fingerling catfish (small catfish fried whole), plus catfish fillets and frog legs, both available fried, Cajun-seasoned, or broiled with lemon pepper. We opted for the Fried Marinated Alligator Bites, which came with a tangy honey-mustard dipping sauce.

Celebration

The Columbia Restaurant, 649 Front Street, Celebration 34747; (407) 566-1505; columbiarestaurant.com. See main listing on p. 115.

Cocoa

Old Florida Grill & Oyster House,
5370 US Highway 1, Cocoa 32927; (321)
735-8979. Old Florida Grill & Oyster
House, a US Highway 1 road house south
of Cape Canaveral, is probably a good
spot to watch a rocket launch. It backs up
to the Indian River about 10 miles south
of Kennedy Space Center. At first I was
put off by a place with "Oyster House" in
its name, and they had to tell me, "Sorry,
we're out of oysters," but I tried the fresh-
catch grilled wahoo sandwich, which was
good.

Daytona Beach

Crabby Joe's, 3701 South
Atlantic Avenue, Daytona
Beach 32118; (386) 756-4219;
sunglowpier.com. The Sun
Glow Pier, which juts out 900
feet into the Atlantic Ocean on
South Daytona Beach, opened
in 1960. Unlike the other "city"
piers, the Sun Glow is privately
owned. Although it has
always had some sort of snack
concession, the Crabby Joe's
Restaurant that is there today

opened in the mid-1980s. Good fresh seafood served in large portions in
a beach-boardwalk open-air atmosphere is Crabby Joe's main draw. My

lunch platter of spicy steamed peel-and-eat shrimp was delicious, and it came with buttered corn on the cob. They also have steamed snow crab legs, steamed mussels, and fried seafood platters with flounder, coconut shrimp, or clam strips. If you don't want something fried, they also have grilled or blackened mahimahi, yellowfin tuna, and shrimp.

Leesburg

Magnolia Oyster Bar, 201 West Magnolia Street, Leesburg 34748; (352) 323-0093; leesburgeats.com/mag.php. Locals in Leesburg call it "the Mag," and it traces its roots all the way back to 1954 as a biker bar. A bit tamer in its current iteration, they are still a bar but better known for their fresh oysters: half-shell raw or fried. There's also steamed clams with garlic butter, and at least one oddball appetizer: fried pickle chips.

Mount Dora

Pisces Rising, 239 West 4th Avenue, Mount Dora 32757; (352) 385-2669; piscesrisingdining.com. Pisces Rising opened in 2004 and sits 2 blocks west of the center of activity on Mount Dora's main avenue, Donnelly Street. From their open-air back deck, diners have a perfect view out over scenic

Lake Dora. Their menu mixes Caribbean/Cuban (Cuban yellowtail snapper), Spanish (seafood paella), and Cajun (jambalaya) with Florida Cracker (shrimp-and-grits). They always have daily specials, and I had their flavorful, cheesy scallops gnocchi, a variation of one of their menu standards, potato gnocchi. They have some spicy appetizers too: crab fritters, Mussels and Clams Gandia in garlic, butter, and white wine with chorizo sausage, and fried calamari tossed in sesame seeds, ponzu, and cherry tomato sauce.

New Smyrna Beach

Barracuda's Bar & Grille, 203 South Atlantic Avenue, New Smyrna Beach 32169; (386) 957-3931; barracudasnsb.com. When the local constable recommends her favorite local beachside dive for seafood, I listen. She did not steer me wrong. I had Barracuda's half pound of big, plump steamed shrimp with blackening seasoning, which gives it a little more kick than the standard Old Bay. This is a great little open-air bar and grill that opened in 2012 right across from New Smyrna's public beach, with sand on the floor and salt in the air. You can also get Mediterranean mussels or clams in white wine garlic sauce; mahi carpaccio ceviche-style with lime, capers, and onions; Maryland crab cakes; fried calamari; their Peninsula paella; or their fresh catch baked in mojo sauce.

JB's Fish Camp, 859 Pompano Avenue, New Smyrna Beach 32169; (386) 427-5747; jbsfishcamp.com. Follow Highway A1A south down the coast from New Smyrna Beach and eventually you will reach the gate to Canaveral National Seashore and 24 miles of some of Florida's most

pristine coastline. But just before you get to that gate, to the right on the Mosquito Lagoon side, you'll see JB's Fish Camp. Captain John "J. B." Bollman opened the Turtle Mound Raw Bar here in the late 1970s, serving fresh clams, oysters, shrimp, and crabs. The shrimp and crabs were live and kept in tanks. Enough regulars had been calling it JB's Fish Camp that he eventually changed the name. The menu grew, and the restaurant grew, and JB's became the local legend that it is today.

John Bollman was an avid fisherman and an avid conservationist, with a degree in biology. He was particularly passionate about preserving Mosquito Lagoon and the Indian River. Sadly Bollman lost his battle with cancer in August 2015. My most recent visit was just a month after his death. He would be happy to know that the place was packed and bustling, and my oysters on the half shell were salty-fresh and delicious. JB's menu has grown to include Grouper ala JB, a casserole with vegetables, corn on the cob, and covered with a white wine cheese sauce; the Shipwreck Special, a casserole of shrimp, scallops, and crab; shrimp or scallop scampi; charbroiled shrimp kebab; and grouper, mahi, shrimp, or alligator seared blackened in a cast-iron skillet.

Norwood's Restaurant, 400 2nd Avenue, New Smyrna Beach 32169; (386) 428-4621; norwoods.com. The coolest thing about Norwood's is the cool and breezy open-air bar. It occupies a 40-foot-high tree house that Robinson Caruso would be envious of. Norwood's has been here since 1946, and while they have a generous seafood menu, their claim to fame is their substantial wine cellar with more than 30,000 bottles. I dined up in the tree house and had a fine grilled swordfish sandwich drizzled with a beurre blanc sauce. Norwood's dinner offerings include shrimp-and-grits with andouille sausage and étouffée sauce, scallops and shrimp Alfredo, seafood

pesto, crab cakes, snow crab legs, and Maine lobster tails. They also offer their fresh catch fish grilled, blackened, or broiled with pineapple chutney or mango salsa, or baked and stuffed with blue crab.

Off the Hook Raw Bar and Grill, 747 3rd Avenue, New Smyrna Beach 32169; (386) 402-9300; offthehookrawbar.com. Once you step inside Off the Hook Raw Bar and Grill, you'll forget you're in a shopping plaza. There's a Hawaiian deep-sea-fishing theme going on here. The menu has all the usual platters: grouper, shrimp, oysters, and mahi, but they have a few more exotic Hawaiian-inspired items too. I tried a refreshing tuna poke, with cubes of fresh raw tuna, avocado, and macadamia nuts, on sticky rice. They also do some Louisiana-inspired dishes like their Creole Boil with steamed oysters, shrimp, snow crab, crawfish, and andouille sausage, and crawfish étouffée.

The Seashack, 491 East 3rd Avenue, New Smyrna Beach 32169; (386) 428-8850; nsbseashack.com. Sometimes you just can't judge a joint by what it looks like out front. In the case of the Seashack, judge it instead by the back, where they have a great rustic open-air bar and deck that overlooks the Callalisa Creek. I started with their seared ahi tuna, generously crusted with pepper, and then finished up with a bucket of steamed oysters, while watching flocks of water fowl gliding over the creek. They also offer something they call Beach Buckets, seafood served steaming hot in a rustic steel bucket with corn on the cob and red potatoes. You can get it with clams, Maine lobster, shrimp, or the Bayou Boil version with shrimp, crawfish, and andouille sausage. Or if you're feeding a crowd, try the Seven Seas Bucket with a dozen oysters, a dozen clams, a dozen mussels, a pound of shrimp, a pound of snow crab legs, a pound of crawfish, and a Maine lobster.

Oak Hill

Goodrich Seafood Restaurant and Oyster House, 253 River Road, Oak Hill 32759; (386) 345-3397; goodrichseafoodandoysterhouse.com. There is a sparsely populated stretch of nether land between Titusville and New Smyrna. At about the halfway point, the Oak Hill Flea Market marks the spot where you can turn east and wind your way over to the western shore of Mosquito Lagoon on the Indian River. Past some trailer parks and boat-repair shops, you will come to the Goodrich Seafood Restaurant (often referred to as simply Goodrich's).

Goodrich's has been here, virtually unchanged, overlooking Mosquito Lagoon since 1971, but its beginnings go much further back. Two brothers, Clarence and Jeff Goodrich, started a wholesale crab business here in 1910, processing and selling blue crabs. There is inside seating, but if the weather cooperates, most patrons sit out back at picnic tables on the dock. Plano tackle boxes at each table contain an assortment of condiments and cocktail sauces. I don't know why it is that the best seafood places always seem to be the farthest off the beaten path, but that adage is certainly confirmed with Goodrich's. I started with a cup of their thick, savory Corn and Crab Chowder. There was so much on the menu that sounded appetizing that I couldn't make up my mind what I wanted for the main course. So I got the Grilled Seafood Platter, with everything: crab cakes, succulent baby bay scallops, grilled oysters, grilled shrimp, and that day's fresh-catch black drum. It was all positively heavenly. People are going to ask

me what my favorite of all the seafood places was, and Goodrich's will be a contender, for sure.

On an interesting side note, former Miami Dolphins football player Larry Csonka purchased the Goodrich Seafood Restaurant building and surrounding property in 2004. Karyn McNamara, with Galbreath Restaurant Group out of Port Orange, actually owns and operates the restaurant today.

Orlando

Lee & Rick's Oyster Bar, 5621 Old Winter Garden Road, Orlando 32811; (407) 293-3587; leeandricksoysterbar.com. Leah and Rick Richter opened Lee & Rick's Oyster Bar in 1950. They had just 9 stools at the bar and there was no menu. All they served was oysters. Rick would drive up to get them in Apalachicola every week. Leah and Rick's son Gene runs Lee & Rick's today, but you get the feeling that this place is a time capsule,

unchanged for over half a century. There is other seafood on the menu now (so they do have a menu now), but people still come here primarily for the fresh oysters.

It's a bit dark inside, but there are lights above the well-worn 80-foot-long concrete bar. Squirt bottles filled with lemon juice sit out on the countertop. I told the woman behind the bar that I'd like 2 dozen. No need for trays, she just shucked oysters and placed them right in front of me. When I was finished, she said, "Just push the shells over the edge of the bar."

Norman's at the Ritz-Carlton, 4012 Central Florida Parkway, Orlando 32837; (407) 393-4333; normans.com. Norman Van Aken, perhaps Florida's most famous and most progressive chef, was exploring and combining cooking styles and flavors from an eclectic assortment of ethnicities long before anybody had ever heard the terms "Floribbean" or "fusion food." In fact, he's credited with inventing the concept, but he prefers the term "New World Cuisine."

Van Aken first showed up in Key West in 1971. He would come and go intermittently in the early years, but the Keys kept pulling him back. Initially he worked at some of the dives and then later at some of the better

joints, like Chez Nancy and Mira at the Marquesa Hotel (which he opened in 1988). But it was his tenure at Louie's Backyard (see Key West section), starting in 1985, that really put both Louie's and Van Aken on the map. Key West was, and still is, both a geographical and cultural crossroads, and that has had a profound influence on its food. Here, Floridian, Caribbean, Central and South American, and Bahamian cuisines collide, and that's what Norman Van Aken's New World Cuisine is all about.

Van Aken's first Norman's opened in 1995 in Coral Gables, and this Norman's at the Ritz Carlton at Grande Lakes in Orlando opened in 2004. The entrance is discreetly tucked away off the hotel's lobby. But once inside, you step into an elegant high-ceiling dining room with windows that wrap around in a semicircle and overlook the hotel's lush gardens, lake, and golf course. It's a fitting setting for some of Florida's most spectacular food. I have had Norman's savory Serrano ham–crusted sea bass with chorizo sausage-saffron risotto, and also (my favorite, and one that he considers a signature dish) his pan-cooked Florida yellowtail snapper fillet with a sweet citrus-butter sauce. The menu shifts with the seasons, but you will likely find these tapas and appetizers on the menu any time: Key West Shrimp Ceviche, Yuca-Stuffed Crispy Shrimp with a mojo-habanero tartar sauce, Lemongrass Marinated Seared Tuna, and Creamy Cracked Conch Chowder.

Van Aken has put Chef Andres Mendoza in charge of his kitchen. Mendoza moved from Puerto Vallarta, Mexico, with his family when he was 20. He began working as a dishwasher at the Marriott Hotel, but his cooking talents quickly moved him up. He attended the Le Cordon Bleu College of Culinary Arts, then worked at several Orlando restaurants before he was hired as Norman's chef de partie. He is now the executive chef.

Palm Bay

Ozzie's Crab House, 4391 Dixie Highway, Palm Bay 32905; (321) 724-0009; ozziescrabhouse.net. When Arthur Alexander opened the original Ozzie's Crab House in Grant-Valkaria (just south of Palm Bay) in 1968, live blue crabs right out of the Indian River Lagoon were their mainstay. That's still the case today, although they also have Dungeness, snow crab, and king crab legs on the menu now too. The current Palm Bay location was being remodeled when I visited, so I ate in their smaller bar next door. I had grilled crab cakes (made with fresh blue crab, of course). Ozzie's likes to keep it simple and let the crab be the star, so their cakes are made just with crabmeat and a little onion and celery, just like I like them. Ozzie's also serves grouper and mahimahi blackened, grilled, fried, or broiled;

seared ahi tuna; shrimp scampi; bacon-wrapped scallops; and lobster Alfredo.

Ponce Inlet

Down the Hatch, 4894 Front Street, Ponce Inlet 32127; (386) 761-4831; down-the-hatch-seafood.com. To find some of the best places to eat, you have to have access to local knowledge. Good friend Gary Katuin, from nearby Lake Helen, first introduced me to Down the Hatch 15 years ago. (Gary also put me on to Aunt Catfish's.) It's a little off the beaten path. When you see the 175-foot-tall historic Ponce Inlet Lighthouse (tallest in Florida and second-tallest in the United States), you know you're close.

Down the Hatch fronts on the Halifax River around the corner from Ponce Inlet, which opens onto the Atlantic. The restaurant had its genesis in Timmons Fish Camp, which opened in 1948 and was run by Ponce Inlet's second mayor B. G. Timmons. His son Frank began operating fishing charters out of the fish camp in the early 1960s, which led to adding offices. Later they added a fish market, and then a pub called the Hatch. Sometime around 1975 they started serving sandwiches, and by 1977 Down the Hatch was officially a restaurant. It's almost two restaurants now. There's a full indoor restaurant with bar, plus more restaurant seating and an additional bar, all on the docks overlooking the river. They have a great selection of fresh seafood, including some inventive dishes like Black and Bleu Tuna blackened with melted bleu cheese, and barbecued fish catch of the day glazed with apricot barbecue sauce. Triggerfish was the "catch" on my most recent visit. I had it as a sandwich, blackened. Triggerfish meat is light and sweet-tasting, which works well with blackening, and Down the Hatch did it right. They also offer Triggerfish St. John with Parmesan cheese, scallions, and tomatoes, beer-batter fried haddock fish-and-chips, smoked salmon smothered in Gouda cheese sauce, broiled Bahamian lobster tails, coconut shrimp, fried clam strips, scallops (fried, blackened, or broiled), and spicy Spanish snapper.

Port Orange

Aunt Catfish's on the River, 4009 Halifax Drive, Port Orange 32127; (386) 767-4768; auntcatfishontheriver.com. If you're eating at a place called Aunt Catfish's, you have to order the catfish. And I was glad I did. I had it grilled and seasoned with lemon-pepper over cheese grits, and it

was superb. As a bonus it comes with a melt-in-your-mouth fresh-baked cinnamon bun. This location at the foot of the Halifax River Bridge was originally a bait-tackle-beer-and-coffee shop called Dave's Dock. Aunt Catfish's opened here in 1979.

This is really good seafood with a Southern accent. How does a lobster grilled cheese sandwich sound? To go with it, try some fried alligator with a citrus dipping sauce, or fried Cajun shark bites. They also have a mix-and-match design-your-own seafood platter. Choose from pan-sautéed garlic shrimp, fried shrimp, coconut shrimp, fried oysters, fried alligator, fried catfish fingerlings, grilled Maryland crab cakes, fried Dijon-sautéed bay scallops, fried Cajun shark bites, or fried frog legs. But if you came for the namesake catfish, you can order it grilled with lemon-pepper (like I did), blackened, Carolina-style fried with salt and pepper, grilled with Cajun spices, or pecan-crusted. And did I mention the fresh-baked cinnamon buns?

Rockledge

River Rocks Restaurant, 6485 US Highway 1, Rockledge 32955; (321) 757-7200; riverrocksrestaurant.com. River Rocks sits on the Indian River Lagoon side of US Highway 1, about halfway between Melbourne Beach and Cape Canaveral. They have two dining venues: the River Rocks dining room, which serves dinner only, and their outdoor Dockside bar, which serves lunch and dinner. I chose Dockside for the idyllic view of the river and had their seared scallops with a side of Brussels sprouts, a simple but tasty dish that hit the spot. They also offer a light-fried crab cake dinner, 2 seafood platters (grilled or fried), and filet mignon and lobster. The River

Rocks dining room menu adds pan seared mahi, whole fried snapper, sesame-seared tuna, and shrimp and scallop Oscar. They also have some tempting starters: conch salad with lime, habanero, red onion, tomato, bell peppers, and cilantro; Crab Stack with lump crab, avocado, mango, arugula, and orange vinaigrette; wild mussels in garlic, tomato, white wine, and lemon broth; and a lobster cocktail.

Titusville

Dixie Crossroads Seafood Restaurant, 1475 Garden Street, Titusville 32796; (321) 268-5000; dixiecrossroads.com. The 1980s through the 1990s was the heyday of NASA's Space Shuttle program, and Titusville was (and still is) NASA-town. Right at the launch of that era, in 1983, boatbuilder and commercial shrimper Rodney Thompson opened Dixie Crossroads Seafood Restaurant. Rock shrimp were most plentiful, and it was Rodney's daughter Laurilee who figured out the best way to cook them: split, buttered, and broiled. So Rodney built a high-speed shrimp-splitting machine, and shrimp became Dixie Crossroads' specialty.

Under Laurilee Thompson's tutelage, Dixie Crossroads has expanded, both in size and in menu offerings. Here's one of my favorite things about Dixie Crossroads: Every meal starts with a basket of hot corn fritters (not hush puppies) coated with powdered sugar. Now there's also local-caught grouper, tilefish, mahi, lobster, and salmon on the menu (all from their own World Ocean Seafood Market, also in Titusville), but I had to have shrimp. I started with their Thai-seasoned Coconut Corn Shrimp Chowder, and then dug into a plate of fresh boiled white shrimp. Of course I also inhaled my basket of sugar-dusted corn fritters (see recipe in "In the Kitchen" section).

Laurilee Thompson isn't just the restaurant owner. She spent a number of years operating commercial fishing and shrimping boats and knows that end of the business quite well. She recognized early on that bottom trawling was damaging the reefs and decimating the area's shrimp population. She became one of the most outspoken and active advocates for conservation, and helped devise plans to protect the sustainability of the shrimping industry.

Vero Beach

Ocean Grill, 1050 Sexton Plaza (Beachland Boulevard), Vero Beach 32963; (772) 231-5409; ocean-grill.com. This is Waldo Sexton's original beachfront Ocean Grill. Sexton was fond of wood structures and built the restaurant with mahogany floors and paneling, and pecky cypress ceilings.

During World War II it served as an officers' club for the nearby naval air base. It would change hands only twice since then. Mary Ellen and Jake Replogle had been operating a burger and hot dog diner in Milwaukee, Wisconsin, when they moved to Vero Beach and purchased the Ocean Grill in 1965. The Replogle family (third generation) still owns and runs it today.

I arrived just before they opened for lunch at 11:30 and got a window seat. Good thing that I arrived early. By 11:45 they were nearly full. I had the Maine lobster roll, with big whole chunks of lobster claw meat (that's the most tender), just lightly mixed with mayonnaise and parsley. Their dinner menu has a wide assortment of savory entrees, including Coquilles St. Jacques Seafood Casserole and Broiled Jumbo Lump Crab Cakes with Mango Salsa. And their selection of appetizers includes their own

Waldo Sexton

Any discussion of Vero Beach history has to include Waldo Sexton. The Indiana native first came to Florida in 1914 and opened his own citrus grove in Indian River County in 1917. But Sexton was a Renaissance man, not content to do just one thing. Soon he had branched out into civic organization, property development, and tourism. In 1932 Sexton and landowner Arthur McKee partnered to open McKee Jungle Gardens, a tropical park filled with exotic flora, on 80 acres just south of Vero Beach. They hired landscape architect William Lyman Phillips, with Frederick Law Olmsted's firm, to design the gardens, one of Florida's earliest tourist attractions. McKee Jungle Gardens survived until the mid-1970s when it closed, but in 1994 the Indian River Land Trust purchased the remaining 18 acres and in 2001 opened McKee Botanical Garden.

In the 1920s Sexton cleared a road (Beachland Boulevard) from Highway A1A east to the beach. In 1935 he built a rambling driftwood residence on the beach, just south of the road, which Mrs. Sexton would convert into the Driftwood Inn a couple years later. It's still there today. In 1941 Sexton built a restaurant, the Ocean Grill, right on the beach at the end of Beachland Boulevard, in the same driftwood style as the inn.

House-Made Smoked Fish Dip; a Cold Shellfish Platter with stone crab claws, jumbo shrimp, and snow crab claws; Steamed Shrimp in Old Bay Seasoning; and Jumbo Lump Crab-Stuffed Mushroom Caps.

On a side note, from my beach-facing window seat, I could see a flag pole straight out from the restaurant, a few hundred yards offshore, that marks the location of the *Breconshire*, a 300-foot-long British steamship that sunk here in 1894. At low tide the bow just peaks out above the surface.

Winter Park

Lombardi's Seafood, 1888 West Fairbanks Avenue, Winter Park 32789; (407) 628-3474; lombardis.com. Owner Tony Lombardi Jr. opened this Lombardi's Seafood in 2006, but he grew up in my hometown of Tampa, where he worked in his father's seafood market. In the early 1960s Tony

Lombardi Sr. moved the business to Winter Park. Tony Jr. bought it in 2006. The market sells a vast variety of seafood: all the usual grouper, mahi, salmon, and tuna, but also corvina, monkfish, orange roughy, and whole rainbow trout. Plus they have specialty items like crawfish, frog legs, and eel. One end of the market is taken up with tables for the cafe. Order at the counter and they'll prepare it fresh. I had the Snapper Minuta, a pan-fried snapper sandwich, and it was perfect.

Winter Park Fish Company, 761 Orange Avenue, Winter Park 32789; (407) 622-6112; thewinterparkfishco.com. It turns out Winter Park Fish Company's faux-fish-shack decor isn't all that faux. The wood tables are actually made from salvaged timber submerged in the St. Johns River during Hurricane Charley, and the wall art is all authentic and by local artists. The place has a comfy, old-bait-shack kind of feel, but the food is a few notches upscale from that. They start each morning with fresh, whole fish (so they can tell just how fresh it is) and fillet them in-house. Sure, they have raw oysters, fish and shrimp tacos, and po'boys. But they also have creative specials like Cioppino Italian Seafood Stew, Grouper Milanese, and Applewood Bacon-Wrapped and Cheese-Stuffed Grouper Cheeks, or anything fresh-catch curry roasted or macadamia-and-coconut-fried. Owner Craig Tremblay (former owner of Winter Park restaurant Bonefish Billy's) opened Winter Park Fish Company in 2010.

Southwest

Up until the late 1970s, St. Petersburg was I-75's southern terminus. To continue from there down the southwest coast and over to Miami meant winding along US Highway 41, which took the better part of a day. The good thing about that was that it kept high-volume traffic from flowing over to some of southwest Florida's most charming and historic small coastal towns, like Boca Grande, Sanibel, and Captiva, in addition to midsize towns like Fort Myers and Naples. By the time I-75 was completed south to Naples in the late 1980s, those small villages had already figured out how valuable their isolation and charm were and had taken measures to restrict excessive development. And while much expansion has taken place in southwest Florida, Boca Grande, Sanibel, and Captiva are nearly as tranquil today as they were 50 years ago. Similarly, Goodland, Everglades City, and Ochopee have been left alone. A hundred years ago these were mostly fishing villages, and today they have not forgotten that heritage. You'll find outstanding seafood at places like Sunshine Seafood Cafe in Captiva, Doc Ford's Rum Bar and Grille in Sanibel, Temptations in Boca Grande, and Joanie's Blue Crab Cafe in Ochopee.

Boca Grande

Eagle Grille, Miller's Dockside Bar and Grill, 220 Harbor Drive, Boca Grande 33921; (941) 979-6995; eaglegrille.com. Miller's Marina has been a Boca Grande icon for decades. While the marina itself is gone, the boat docks remain, and it makes a classic waterfront setting for Miller's Dockside and its upstairs cousin, the Eagle Grille Restaurant. I had lunch at a table at the outdoor Miller's Dockside, close enough to the water that I could toss the tails from my very tasty peel-and-eat shrimp into the water to feed snook schooling among the yachts and fishing boats. Miller's Dockside serves tasty tuna nachos, calamari fritto, and steamed mussels in onion garlic butter as appetizers. Dinner favorites include bronzed, blackened, or amandine grouper; Gasparilla Shrimp and Grits; and shrimp, scallops, and grouper seafood platter. The upstairs Eagle Grille offers a similar menu but with a few upscale additions, like seared Thai scallops in nori-soy-sake butter, Boca Macadamia Shrimp in Rum Mango Sauce, and peppercorn-crusted ahi tuna with pineapple-soy glaze.

Remote Islands in Florida

Remote Florida tropical islands, reachable by car, are an increasingly rare commodity. Sanibel and Captiva Islands, off the coast of Fort Myers, are hardy holdouts. To get any more remote, you will need a boat or a seaplane, or you'll need to be an exceptionally good swimmer. The islands' first permanent settlers arrived in the late 19th century, but a hundred years before, they had been the hunting grounds and hideaways of pirates.

Sanibel is famous for its gorgeous, shell-strewn beaches and chic boutiques, and you'll drive through it to get to even more remote Captiva. The two are connected by a short bridge that spans Blind Pass. Captiva is a bit more tropical and a bit less populated. Dense flora—sea grapes, frangipani, crotons, spiny aloe, and all varieties of palm including sable, coconut, royal, butterfly, and cabbage—populate the island. No surprise, there is exceptionally good food to be found on both islands.

Six-mile-long Gasparilla Island and the village of Boca Grande are only accessible by a single toll bridge at its north end, or by boat or seaplane. This relative isolation has allowed it to develop a tranquil, tropical, laid-back personality. There are no stoplights, and the only structure more than 3 stories tall is a steel-girder 1927 lighthouse tower (still functioning) on the southern beach. Tin-roofed bungalows nestled among ghostly banyan trees make up the surrounding neighborhood, originally developed in the 1890s by Albert Gilchrist, who would later become Florida's 20th governor.

Temptations, 350 Park Avenue, Boca Grande 33921; (941) 964-2610; temptationbocagrande.com. Temptations' dining room and tiny fisherman's bar next door have likely not changed one bit since they opened in 1947. This place is a veritable time capsule. At some point they did add a second dining room in the back, which they call the Caribbean Room. Another thing that has not changed is Temptations' excellent food.

It's also pricey, but then again you are in Boca Grande on Gasparilla Island, where it costs $6 just to cross the bridge onto the island. My most recent meal here was an outstanding Bronzed Hogfish, with meunière sauce. Despite being stuffed, I topped off dinner with a colossal piece of their homemade coconut cake. Temptations' lobster corn chowder is another favorite of mine. Other regular dinner entrees include crabmeat au gratin; fried or sautéed soft-shell crabs; New Orleans spicy fried shrimp; pan-fried snapper in lemon, garlic, and apple juice; and various combo dishes with grouper, shrimp, oysters, and soft-shell crab.

Captiva and Sanibel

Doc Ford's Rum Bar and Grille, 975 Rabbit Road, Sanibel 33957; (239) 472-8311; docfordssanibel.com. Before he was a popular novelist, Randy Wayne White was a much in demand charter light-tackle fishing guide working the waters in and around Pine Island Sound, Boca Grande,

Cayo Costa, Captiva, and Sanibel. He knows fish, particularly local fish. So perhaps it was a natural progression for him to eventually end up in the seafood restaurant business. Doc Ford's Rum Bar & Grille (named for Randy Wayne White's adventure-mystery series protagonist) opened in 2003 as a joint venture with a couple other investors, and like White's other endeavors, it has been a resounding success. Many patrons come the first time because they're Randy Wayne White fans, but they come the second time (and third and fourth . . .) because the food is outstanding. Doc Ford's menu leans toward the tropical, Central and South American, Cuban, and Caribbean. I have several regular favorites: Banana Leaf Snapper, Island Style Shrimp and Grits, and then the one thing I have to get every single time: Yucatan Shrimp, which is steamed peel-and-eat shrimp in a spicy chili, cilantro, garlic, key lime juice, and butter sauce. It comes with fresh-baked crusty French bread to soak up the remaining sauce after the shrimp have been devoured. You can also snack on steamed mussels in roasted garlic, shallots, tomatoes, and basil; pan-fried Captiva crab cakes; and fried calamari; plus raw or steamed oysters and ceviche. And you can dine on mahimahi seared in a sweet soy sauce; cedar plank salmon, Oriental panko-crusted grouper; seafood paella; and Island-Style Shrimp and Grits, with shrimp dusted in Mexican masa corn flour and jalapeño cheese grits.

The Sanibel location is the original, but they've opened two more since, one on Captiva (near the entrance to South Seas Plantation) and one in Fort Myers.

Sunshine Seafood Cafe, 14900 Captiva Drive, Captiva 33924; (239) 472-6200; captivaislandinn.com/facilities/sunshine-seafood-cafe-wine-bar. The Sunshine Seafood Cafe is a lasting Captiva favorite. In 2003 it was purchased by Fort Myers restaurateur Sandra Stilwell, who also owns Captiva Inn plus several other restaurants on Captiva and in Fort Myers. She remodeled, doubling the seating space, but best of all kept the wonderful wood-grilled Pan-Asian/Floribbean/Italian entrees on the menu. I am partial to the yellowfin tuna au poivre with a piquant red wine and pepper demi-glace sauce. Their pan-seared red snapper piccata is second on my list. Some other wonderful entrees include Wood Grilled "Blind Pass" Jumbo Shrimp with Orange Blossom Honey Barbeque Sauce, pan-sautéed jumbo lump crab cakes, paella, and Prince Edward Island Mussels Herbanato sautéed in white wine, garlic, lemon juice, and butter.

Everglades City

City Seafood Market and Restaurant, 702 Begonia Street, Everglades City 34139; (239) 695-4700; cityseafood1.com. Some of Everglades City's best seafood can be found in this unlikely appearing ramshackle building sitting on the banks of the Barron River. In addition to the more conventional grouper, oysters, scallops, and shrimp, City Seafood serves

Everglades City and the Tamiami Trail

From Highway 41, better known as the Tamiami Trail, Everglades National Park seems to be just an endless expanse of saw grass, slash pine bay heads, and swamp. But a closer look reveals that it's brimming with wildlife. Over 300 species of birds call the Everglades home; among them, ospreys, bald eagles, blue herons, great egrets, wood ibis, anhingas, pink roseate spoonbills, and purple gallinules. One of the rarest, the Everglades snail kite lives here too.

Everglades City had been a sleepy fishing village and trading outpost until 1923 when New York advertising magnate Barron Collier made it his headquarter's town from which construction operations for the Tampa-to-Miami "Tamiami" Trail took place. Original construction on the "Trail" had first begun in 1915, but by 1922 the State of Florida ran out of funds needed to complete the last section from Naples to Miami. Collier had made millions with his New York City Consolidated Street Railway Advertising Company and was reinvesting his earnings in southwest Florida real estate. By the early 1920s he had accumulated over a million acres, making him the largest single landowner in the state at that time. The Tamiami Trail would be crucial to the appreciation of Collier's real estate holdings, so he proposed an idea to the state: If they would divide Lee County and create a new southern county (which they would name "Collier"), he would finance and oversee the completion of the trail. It took 5 years of digging, dredging, and dynamiting, but on April, 26, 1928, the Tamiami Trail officially opened.

After Hurricane Donna thrashed Everglades City in 1960, Collier pulled the last of his interests out of the town. The county seat moved to Naples, and Everglades City settled back into the quiet fishing village that it once was and still is today.

some delightful Everglades delicacies: fried frog legs, cracked conch, soft-shell blue crab, and gator tail, which you know is fresh because there are alligators everywhere down here!

Marco Island

Little Bar Restaurant, 205 Harbor Drive, Goodland on Marco Island 34145; (239) 394-5663; littlebarrestaurant.com. A block up the road from Stan's, you'll find the Little Bar Restaurant. The sign says "New Little Bar and Restaurant," but most of the decorations and accoutrements inside are relics salvaged from old bars around the country by Little Bar founder Ray Bozicnik, which makes the place interesting to browse through. Bozicnik opened Little Bar in 1978, and his son Ray operates it today. Fresh stone crab claws (in season), grouper, tuna, swordfish, mahi, snapper, and blue-crab cakes are regular menu items. For appetizers check out their Smoked Amberjack Spread and their Grouper Balls (who knew?).

Stan's Idle Hour Bar and Seafood Restaurant, 221 Goodland Drive, Goodland on Marco Island 34145; (239) 394-3041; stansidlehour.net. To keep the occasional visitor and the few locals watered and fed, Goodland has two bar and grills, both with good local fresh seafood. The first one you come to is Stan's Idle Hour. Owner Stan Gober was Goodland's Renaissance man: restaurateur, singer-songwriter, stand-up comic, and festival promoter. Stan's Idle Hour has been hosting Goodland's Annual Mullet Festival every January since the 1980s. The event culminates

Goodland

The tiny fishing community of Goodland (population 267 as of the 2010 census) sits tucked away on the edge of the Ten Thousand Islands, in striking contrast to Marco Island's high-rise Gulf-front beach condos 5 miles away. A handful of homesteaders settled here at "Goodland Point" back in the late 1800s. Then a few more came after the first Goodland bridge, an old wooden swing bridge, was built in 1935. Not too much has changed since then, and that's the way folks here like it. What it lacks in size, it makes up for in personality.

in the crowning of that year's Buzzard Lope Queen. "Buzzard Lope" is named for a Stan Gober song and the local's favorite dance. Sadly Stan passed away in 2012, but his legend lives on. They recently renamed the bridge over to Goodland the Stan Gober Memorial Bridge, and they've added a Stan look-alike contest to their annual Lobsterfest in March. Stan's offers a wide assortment of fresh seafood platters, fried, blackened, broiled, and sautéed: shrimp, catfish, oysters, frog legs, scallops, and soft-shell crab. If you can't make up your mind, try the Captain's Platter or the even larger Stan's Ultimate Platter. They'll also happily cook what you catch and bring them.

Naples

Avenue 5, 699 5th Avenue South, Naples 34102; (239) 403-7170; avenue5naples.com. Fifth Avenue is Naples upscale Main Street, in some ways like Palm Beach's Worth Avenue but not quite as, well . . . snooty. Naples has always prided itself on having all the elegance of Palm Beach but without the attitude. Inn on 5th is 5th Avenue's quite elegant boutique hotel, with 119 rooms and one of Naples best restaurants, Avenue 5. The location was a 1950s bank building that had seen better days, until the mid-1990s when Boston-born developer Phil McCabe purchased it and began converting it into a hotel. He also wanted an adjoining restaurant and decided on a theme to match his Irish heritage. He actually went to Dublin in 1997 to purchase authentic fixtures and materials and to hire real Irish craftsmen to come back to Naples and build his McCabe's Irish Pub and Grill. McCabe's Pub quickly became one of Naples most popular nightspots.

In 2012 he had just finished a complete remodel of Inn on 5th and decided it was time for a change for the restaurant too. This time he hired New York interior design firm Jeffery Beers International to create a sophisticated but inviting space to match the restaurant's equally sophisticated, primarily seafood, menu. And about that menu: First, there is lobster, 7 different ways: baked stuffed Maine lobster tail, lobster bisque, lobster Cobb salad, lobster sliders, lobster roll, lobster mac and cheese, and of course lobster surf and turf. Among their additional signature entrees are seafood bouillabaisse with rock shrimp, fish, clams, and mussels in a saffron broth; Deep Sea "Diver" Scallops; ponzu-glazed swordfish; black grouper Oscar; sweet soy yellowfin tuna; cedar-plank Scottish salmon; and then my order: a fabulous, melt-in-your-mouth miso-sake glazed Chilean sea bass with bok choy and udon noodles. This one ranks among the top seafood meals I have eaten while researching this book.

Ochopee

Joanie's Blue Crab Cafe, 39395 Tamiami Trail, Ochopee 34141; (239) 695-2682; joaniesbluecrabcafe.com. Across the highway and down the road a few hundred yards from the Ochopee Post Office, you will find Joanie's Blue Crab Cafe. In 1987 Joanie Griffin and her husband, Carl (now passed away), purchased this old roadside Florida Cracker house, which had previously seen use as a barn and also as an office for an oil company. They turned it into an Everglades diner, but it's as much a museum of swamp eclectia as it is a place to eat. You will be sharing your meal with alligator heads and all manner of taxidermied swamp creatures. As for the menu, Joanie's specializes in things that were swimming (or crawling or hopping) around in the Everglades the day before: frog legs, soft-shell blue crab, and alligator tail. They offer oysters, shrimp, blackened catfish, and

A Tiny Post Office

For driving across the Everglades, I find the Tamiami Trail (Highway 41) slower but much more scenic than Alligator Alley (I-75). I've always got an eye out for a skunk ape, Florida's version of the Bigfoot, or perhaps the even more elusive Florida panther. I have yet to see either, but I'm still hopeful. One thing you can spot (but don't blink or you'll miss it) is the Ochopee Post Office. It's a corrugated-tin shed, hardly bigger than an outhouse, and has the distinction of being the smallest official post office in the United States. The tiny building was originally an irrigation pipe shed for a tomato farm. A 1953 fire burned Ochopee's previous general store and post office to the ground. Postmaster Sidney Brown hurriedly put the pipe shed into what he assumed would be temporary service. But it served its purpose so well that no one saw reason to replace it. Tourists stop here regularly just to get the Ochopee 34141 postmark on their mail.

crab cakes as well. I opted for the Fried Gator Bites Salad, which was a full meal and came with another of Joanie's specialties, crispy, spicy Seminole Indian Fry Bread.

Punta Gorda

Peace River Seafood, 5337 Duncan Road (US Highway 17), Punta Gorda 33982; (941) 505-8440; facebook.com/peace.seafood. Kelly and Jim Beall opened Peace River Seafood in 2003 in a 1927 bungalow that was once a feed store. Your greeter at the front door is Gaspar the parrot. While blue crabs are a specialty (Jim spent a number of years in the crabbing business), they offer an assortment of other old-Florida seafood dishes, like their Thorton Branch Gator Gumbo with shrimp, sausage, crab, and of course fresh gator meat. I went for the Myakka Slew Shrimp Creole with plump shrimp and andouille sausage, corn on the cob, okra, tomatoes, and yellow rice. This is no side item. It's a hearty meal that requires a fork, knife, and spoon to eat. And it beats any shrimp Creole I've eaten in New Orleans. Other regular fresh fish items include mullet, pompano, and snapper, and there's a pretty good chance that Kelly and Jim caught it themselves. Some of Peace River Seafood's "starter plates" are really platters meant for everybody at the table to feast on, and they have catchy names like A Night at Whorehouse Point, which is a steamed platter with a

Alien Invasion in Florida's Waters:
Attack of the Lionfish

The lionfish may be beautiful to look at and quite tasty to eat, but it doesn't belong here. They are native only to the southern Pacific and Indian Oceans, and also the Red Sea. Lionfish began showing up off Florida's Atlantic coast in the mid-1980s, and by 2000 the population had grown dramatically, spreading into the Gulf of Mexico. Venomous barbs along their dorsal and pelvic fins protect them from predators, so they multiply unchecked. As an invasive species, they are voracious consumers of bait fish that native species like snapper and grouper survive on. The Florida Fish and Wildlife Conservation Commission actively encourages people to remove them wherever they are found in Florida waters, mostly around reefs. If you decide to do your part and try to catch one, beware the barbs! In the spirit of doing their part to eradicate these rascals, some restaurants are now cooking and serving lionfish, often as the special of the day. I tried lionfish for the first time at Tamara's Cafe in Apalachicola (see p. 16). They served it pan-fried whole, and it was delicious. Lionfish has a light, flaky meat, similar to snapper or sea bass.

Where do non-native species come from, and how do they get here? Florida, perhaps more than any other state, has a long history of invading species. The Cuban tree frog arrived here in 1931. They were stowaways in the packing material in boxes arriving by boat from Cuba. These guys prey on the smaller native Florida tree frogs. Their population grew rapidly throughout South Florida and they are still here today. In the late 1960s walking catfish began strutting about in South Florida, and by the 1970s they had made their way up to Central Florida. Yes, walking catfish do walk on land. Green iguanas from Central and South America began showing up on Florida's west coast in the 1960s. By the late 1970s the island of Boca Grande was overrun by them. Now Boca Grande traps and removes them. Today iguanas are common in South Florida and particularly in the Keys. While iguanas are not particularly dangerous, there are other more recent invaders that are. Nile monitor lizards, some the length of medium-size alligators, are showing up in South Florida, and 10- to 12-foot-long Burmese pythons have invaded the Everglades as well as the greater Miami area. Iguanas likely arrived on boats from Central and South America, but monitor lizard and python populations originated with released pets and zoo escapes. Some invasive species are not so noticeable. The zebra mussel, and now the green mussel, arrived via ballast water from overseas ships.

Lionfish are an especially troublesome invasive species because they are so resilient. Although they are most commonly found in shallow reefs, they also have been found thriving at depths of 1,000 feet. And they are prodigious reproducers: The female lionfish releases egg masses of 12,000 to 15,000 eggs, which can float and drift for 3 or 4 weeks. Lionfish can spawn every 4 days in warmer climates. Adults grow to 12 to 15 inches, which doesn't sound very big, but they routinely attack and consume other fish that are more than half their size. They stalk their prey and corral them into a corner, then attack. Smaller snapper, grouper, parrotfish, and shrimp are common victims.

While we've been able to trace the sources of many other non-native creatures, how lionfish came here remains a mystery. They first showed up off Florida's Atlantic Coast near Dania Beach in 1985, and now they're found throughout the southern Atlantic and the Gulf of Mexico. The vast majority are red lionfish (*Pterois volitans* for you technical types). They are actually quite striking to look at. They have bold vertical red and white zebra stripes and feather-like fins that extend out to twice the size of their body. But their pretty appearance is a deception. These guys are wreaking havoc in Florida's waters.

So what is being done about them? First, the Florida Fish and Wildlife Conservation Commission, along with a variety of other organizations, are actively educating the public about lionfish and coming up with ways to reduce their population. Florida Fish and Wildlife has waived any fishing license requirement for catching lionfish with a pole spear, or "Hawaiian sling." They want us to catch as many as we can. The only exception is in no-fishing-allowed preserve areas. Lionfish don't bite hooked bait very often, so they are best caught by spearfishing or with dipping nets, but if you do try to catch them with a rod and reel, you'll need a saltwater fishing license. Florida Fish and Wildlife also encourages and issues permits for lionfish fishing tournaments or "derbies." These have caught on. In 2015 there were 31 Florida lionfish derbies, from Pensacola down to the Keys.

pound of shrimp, a dozen clams, and a dozen oysters. They also do grilled or blackened catfish, grouper, and mahi sandwiches; Crabby Girl Kelly's Crab Cakes; and Cudjoe Key Florida Lobster Tails.

Venice

Sharky's on the Pier, 1600 Harbor Drive South, Venice 34285; (941) 488-1456; sharkysonthepier.com. Sharkey's, which opened in 1987, sits right on Venice Beach at the Venice Beach Pier. A thatched roof shades most of the tables in this open-air tiki-themed bar and grill. In 2013 owners Mike and (son) Justin Pachota also added an upstairs, more-upscale dining room called Fins. I had Sharky's delicious Maine lobster roll, with a generous heap of fresh lobster salad on a grilled bun, and I've also had their excellent mahi tacos. Other popular items include jambalaya pasta and something they call Walk the Plank, with layers of grouper, salmon, and mahi baked on a cedar plank with lobster-mushroom sauce. Additional entrees include shrimp-and-chips; Captain's Platter with shrimp, scallops, and grouper; lobster-stuffed flounder; Island Jambalaya with shrimp and andouille sausage; and lobster mac and cheese. The food is consistently good here. Sharky's chefs Marc Alton and Eric Eastes are local multiple Iron Chef Competition winners.

Snook Haven, 5000 East Venice Avenue, Venice 34292; (941) 485-7221; snookhaven.com. Drive 0.75 mile down gravel East Venice Avenue, go through the gate, and eventually you will dead-end into Snook Haven. Their website says it opened in 1948, but the old wooden sign on their riverfront porch, which hangs over a meandering bend in the Myakka River, says 1938. Either way, it's been here for a long time, and back then it may or may not have been a transit point for local moonshiners. Later it became a private fishing camp, and then in 1988 it opened as a fish-and-barbecue joint. It sits on property that has been owned by Sarasota County since 2006, and when the previous operators couldn't make rent, it closed in 2012. Later that year the Pachota family, owners of Sharky's on the Pier in Venice Beach (see above), came along and decided Snook Haven had some potential. So they signed a lease with the county, remodeled the kitchen, spruced the place up a little (but not too much, thankfully), and reopened in February 2013.

When I pulled up on a Thursday for lunch, I expected to be about the only person there. But I was wrong. Thursday is Gulf Coast Banjo Society day and the place was packed with folks sitting outside watching 2 dozen banjo players, plus a couple saxophone players and one accordion player, perform old-time favorites like "Bill Baily" and "Blue Spanish Eyes." It was an unexpected treat and went quite well with my exceptionally tasty iron-pan-seared catfish with collard greens and black-eyed-pea salad. They'll also do the catfish (or tilapia or salmon) fried or blackened. Other seafood items include fish-and-chips, shrimp-and-chips, shrimp po'boys, smoked salmon tacos, fried gator bites, and smoked frog legs. This is one of those places where the food is fabulous and the atmosphere makes it taste even better.

Southeast

It seems unfathomable today that one person could have had so much influence on the development of Florida's entire eastern coastline. But if not for Standard Oil cofounder and railroad tycoon Henry Morrison Flagler, much of that coast and certainly southeast Florida might look quite different today.

Flagler was already in his mid-50s when he came to St. Augustine, Florida, in 1883 on honeymoon with his second wife, Ida. He was enthralled with the town but surprised at the lack of development. Two years later he began construction there on the spectacular 450-room Spanish Renaissance Ponce de Leon Hotel (now Flagler College). By the end of 1889, he had purchased an assortment of small rail lines, connecting and improving them, and added bridges where ferries had done the job before. His railroad now extended as far south as Daytona, and for a while he thought that this was as far as he would go. But in 1892 he acquired the state charter to build railroads down as far south as Miami. Up until now he had bought and improved on existing rails, but this would require building tracks from scratch, much of it through uncharted swamp and wilderness. In Palm Beach he built the Royal Poinciana Hotel, and 2 years later, the Breakers on the beach in front of it. Once again, he did not anticipate going any farther south, but orange-grove owner Julia Tuttle changed all that. Tuttle, who owned considerable acreage in what is now downtown Miami, offered to split her property with Flagler if he would bring his railroad all the way down to Miami. At first Flagler passed on the offer, but 2 years later a devastating February freeze wiped out nearly all of central and north Florida's citrus. Tuttle seized the moment and sent Flagler a cutting of fresh healthy orange blossoms from her groves, along with a reminder that her offer still stood. Oranges were probably the biggest commodity being shipped north on Flagler's rail cars, and Mrs. Tuttle's message hit home this time.

So, an orange grove became Florida's largest and most densely populated city. And Carl Fisher took a mosquito-infested mangrove barrier island and dredged up enough sand to turn it into that city's beach (see Miami Beach introduction). But for us seafood lovers, something great happened when Joseph Weiss began serving stone-crab claws at his restaurant on that beach.

It was a monumental task for Henry Flagler to bring the railroad down to Miami, but one that still wouldn't compare to what he did next: He built the Overseas Railway down to Key West. For that story, see the sidebar "The Florida Keys: How One Man's Crazy Dream Opened the Keys to Everyone."

◆•• ———————— ◆◆•◆ ——————— •••◆

Deerfield Beach

Oceans 234, 234 North Ocean Boulevard, Deerfield Beach 33441; (954) 428-2539; oceans234.com. Danielle Rosse (who also owns the Whale Raw Bar in Parkland; see p. 200) had worked at her mother-in-law's Oceans 234 Restaurant for more than a decade when she decided to buy it and rebuild it in 2013. It already had the perfect location—in the center of Deerfield Beach's action—but it needed a new look. The result is a spectacular venue with indoor and outdoor seating looking out over the beach and the fishing pier. The menu went upscale too: Shrimp and Corn Crusted Snapper, Coriander Dusted Yellowfin Tuna, Pistachio Mahi, lobster mac and cheese, and my choice, Grilled Bronzino. Bronzino is a Mediterranean sea bass, flaky and flavorful. Oceans 234 grills it with just a little olive oil and lemon, and that is all it needs.

Two Georges at the Cove, 1754 Southeast 3rd Court, Deerfield Beach 33441; (954) 421-9272; twogeorgesrestaurant.com/thecove. First, about the name: The original Two Georges Restaurant is in nearby Boynton Beach, so when its owner Steve Scaggs bought the Cove on the Intracoastal Waterway in Deerfield Beach in 2010, he decided to hang on to "the Cove." Scaggs could easily have changed the name, but as a kid growing up here, he often ate at the Cove, so perhaps sentimentality won. So this is a place with a little history and a scenic waterfront location, but it's the food that packs the house every evening.

Two Georges at the Cove's menu is practically a seafood smorgasbord. For appetizers they offer Maryland Crab Dip for scooping with tortilla chips, Bahamian Conch Fritters, Bang Bang Shrimp in a spicy and sweet Thai chili sauce, fried calamari, steamed clams, and Steamed and Spiced Peel and Eat Shrimp. For entrees their fresh-catch choices are usually dolphin (mahimahi), grouper, salmon, and wahoo, blackened or grilled. In addition they list some northeastern-inspired dishes: Maryland crab cakes, Jumbo Crab Norfolk, crab Imperial, and an everything-in-the-kitchen Seafood Pot with shrimp, clams, mussels, calamari, lobster tail, and potatoes in a tomato-garlic broth; plus one Southern-inspired dish: seafood mac and cheese with shrimp, scallops, and crabmeat, penne pasta, 3 types of cheese, and just to make sure it is Southern, bacon. I went for something less complex, the blackened dolphin, which was excellent.

The Whale's Rib Raw Bar, 2031 Northeast 2nd Street, Deerfield Beach 33441; (954) 421-8880; whalesrib.com. The Whale's Rib Raw Bar (not to be confused with the Whale Raw Bar and Fish House in Parkland), a half block off the beach, may look like a hole-in-the-wall, but it's been one of

Deerfield Beach's most popular seafood joints since it opened in 1981. This is a true bar and grill, with booths and barstools, and license-plate-decorated walls, and good food. The menu includes all the standard seafood platter offerings, but their sandwiches are what

most patrons come for: mahi, yellowfin tuna, and tilapia grilled, blackened, or fried, and all served on their fresh-baked whole bun bread. I selected the substantial and savory lobster salad sandwich with homemade potato chips.

Florida Keys

Cudjoe Key

Square Grouper Bar & Grill, 22658 Overseas Highway, Cudjoe Key 33042; (305) 745-8880; squaregrouperbarandgrill.com. Lynn Bell's family summer-vacationed in Marathon when she was growing up in the 1970s, and in 2003 she opened Square Grouper on nearby Cudjoe Key. Some of the Lower "in-between" Keys—Ramrod, Cudjoe, Big Pine, and Sugarloaf—may be sparsely populated, but that does not mean you won't find good food. Square Grouper is a perfect example with dishes like Toasted Almond Encrusted Grouper; seafood stew with shrimp, scallops, and calamari; and Seared Sesamo Encrusted Tuna. By the way, in case you're not already familiar with the term, "square grouper" is not a fish. Back in the early 1970s the Lower Keys were notorious as a drop spot for marijuana smugglers flying up from South and Central America. The smugglers would fly low, often at night, buzzing the ocean mere feet above the waves to avoid radar. At a designated point they would kick the square bails of contraband out an open door over water, where hired fishermen could retrieve the bails. They called it fishing for square grouper.

Islamorada

The Green Turtle Inn, 81219 Overseas Highway, Islamorada 33036; (305) 664-2006; greenturtlekeys.com. In Christopher Columbus's day sea voyagers routinely captured sea turtles and kept them live on-ship. Sea turtles can go months, even a year, without eating anything and survive, and this made them an ideal food source for long voyages. As recently as the 1960s, they were still being harvested as food, but thankfully by the 1970s most and eventually all sea turtle species were declared endangered and protected.

In 1947 Sid and Roxie Siderious bought an Islamorada roadside diner and motel called the Rustic Inn, which had been built in 1928. It was one of the few structures still standing after the Labor Day 1935 Hurricane. The

The Labor Day 1935 Hurricane

Today Islamorada is best known as Florida's big-game Sportfishing Capital. Avid fishing enthusiasts flock to these Upper Keys from around the world to go after blue marlin, sailfish, swordfish, wahoo, tuna, and dolphin (also known as mahi or dorado). Although spring and summer are peak seasons, you can fish here year-round. Legendary sportfishermen like Ernest Hemingway, Zane Grey, and Ted Williams fished these waters and helped make Islamorada famous.

But Islamorada, along with Plantation Key to the north and Lower Matecumbe and Long Keys just south, share a nightmarish chapter in their history. On Labor Day in 1935 the most powerful hurricane ever to strike the continental United States blasted across these islands. It was small in diameter but horrifically potent, cutting across Long and Lower Matecumbe Keys with gusts estimated near 250 mph. A 20-foot tidal wave swept over the islands and ripped whole buildings off their foundations. The people there had almost no warning. On Sunday, the day before it struck, forecasters had called it a mere tropical storm and thought it would likely pass south of Key West.

The Labor Day Hurricane wiped out whole generations of pioneer families (the "Conchs") that had settled the Upper Keys, mostly Russels, Pinders, and Parkers. It also killed hundreds of road workers who were building US Highway 1, all World War I veterans, camped on Lower Matecumbe. In the summer of 1935, the Veterans Administration had employed 680 World War I vets to work on building the Overseas Highway, following Flagler's railway route down to Key West. On that weekend some of the workers had gone to Miami for the holiday, but many stayed behind at their temporary camps. The storm intensified dramatically overnight, and on Monday morning officials called for a train from Miami to evacuate the road workers and residents. The 11-car passenger train reached Islamorada right when the wall of water struck, blasting each of its 100-ton cars right off the tracks. Only the locomotive remained upright. It would be the last train to travel these tracks. The hurricane's death toll exceeded 400 and included all that had remained in the road worker camps, plus entire families of local residents. Months after the storm, remains of victims' bodies were still being recovered. Thirty years later, while dredging on an outlying key near Islamorada, a developer found an automobile with a 1935 license plate and five skeletons inside.

Sideriouses renamed it the Green Turtle Inn, and they specialized in cooking and serving locally fished turtle. The Green Turtle became famous for their turtle steaks and turtle soup. At that time, sea turtles were plentiful in the Keys, and no one thought of them as endangered.

The Sideriouses were energetic entertainers, regularly throwing parties, often with celebrities in attendance. That atmosphere set a Green Turtle Inn standard that would outlive their ownership. The Green Turtle had several subsequent owners through the years, but perhaps the most colorful was Henry "Bastille" Rosenthal, a famous magician who had performed around the world. Rosenthal owned and ran the Green Turtle Inn for several decades, and on occasion he would perform impromptu for his dinner patrons.

Of course today the Green Turtle does not serve sea turtle, however, they do serve farm-raised freshwater snapping turtle. I tried their turtle chowder, a thick, hearty, spicy stew like an Irish stew with turtle meat. It comes with a bottle of pepper sherry if you want to make it even hotter. If turtle is not your thing, there are other spicy dishes: Try the lobster mac and cheese or Southern Smoked Shrimp and Grits, or their Cedar Key Middle Neck Clams in a saffron-tomato broth with chorizo sausage.

Hungry Tarpon Restaurant, 77522 Overseas Highway, Islamorada 33036; (305) 664-0535; hungrytarpon.com. You won't see a sign for the Hungry Tarpon from US Highway 1/A1A. Instead, turn off at the sign for "Robbie's Marina" just across the Lignumvitae Channel Bridge over to Lower Matecumbe Key. Be careful not to run over any of the iguanas that are always sunning here on the side of the road. Park and wander through the open-air bazaar, where artists sell paintings, sculptures, jewelry, and all manner of tropical-themed knickknacks. Robbie's has a kind of hippie-commune feel to it that fits with the Keys. Keep wandering toward the water until you find tables overlooking a dock where people are feeding tarpons by hand, and you're at the Hungry Tarpon. This is the second place where I dined on fish-and-grits for breakfast (the first was at Mrs. Mac's Kitchen; see Key Largo below). My fish was mahi again but this time it was fried, and it came with the requisite bowl of grits, 2 fried eggs, and perhaps the biggest and butteriest biscuit I have ever eaten.

Key Largo

Ballyhoo's, 97860 Overseas Highway, Key Largo 33037; (305) 852-0822; ballyhoosrestaurant.com. Bobby Stoky, who owns Sundowners (see below) also owns and operates Ballyhoo's in this quaint 1930s Conch cottage. Yellowtail snapper features prominently on his menu. There's crabmeat-stuffed yellowtail with béarnaise sauce; Matecumbe yellowtail with an

Italian slant, cooked in tomatoes, scallions, and capers; and Yellowtail Snapper Hemingway, which I happily dined on. It came crusted with Parmesan cheese and key lime butter and was topped with lump crabmeat. They also have charbroiled oysters with a similar topping (but without the crabmeat); buttered poached grilled lobster with key lime butter; and conch meunière with garlic butter, key lime, and Worcestershire. Just for the record, there is no ballyhoo on the menu. The small pointy-nosed ballyhoo is primarily a bait fish, frequently used when trolling for big-game fish, but it makes a catchy (pun intended) name for the restaurant!

The Fish House, 102341 Overseas Highway, Key Largo 33037; (305) 451-0650; fishhouse.com. Doug Prew and C. J. Berwick came to Key Largo in 1987 and bought a small fish house called (you guessed it) the Fish House. Not exactly an inspired name, but they kept it. In 2002 they expanded by buying the property next door, which they called the Fish House Encore. Shrimp features prominently on the appetizer menu: coconut fried, buffalo fried, baked with garlic butter, and Angels on Horseback (baked and wrapped in bacon). There are dinner dish versions of the same, along with several combo platters. But they specialize in several different preparations for their fresh catches: Matecumbe, with an Italian twist including tomatoes, shallots, capers, basil, olive oil, and lemon;

pan sautéed in lemon, butter, and sherry; Hemingway, baked with Italian breadcrumbs and topped with a white wine cream sauce; and Black and Bleu, blackened with a bleu cheese sauce. For lunch I had one of their fresh-catch special sandwiches, a grilled wahoo sandwich. Wahoo is a firm, white, and flavorful fish, and the Fish House grilled it perfectly.

Key Largo Conch House, 100211 Overseas Highway, Key Largo 33037; (305) 453-4844; keylargoconchhouse.com. In 2004 Ted and Laura Deaver bought an existing cafe called Franks, in a house hidden among banyan trees just off US Highway 1/A1A. At first it was just a coffeehouse with some breakfast items. But before long they opened up for lunch and dinner and focused on fresh and sustainable Florida seafood. Today it's a family operation, with their two sons, Justin and Jonathan, and daughter Stephanie all pitching in. They still do breakfast and are known for their seafood Benedicts: cracked conch Benedict, lobster Benedict, shrimp Benedict, and crab cake Benedict. Plus this is the only place I know of that serves a grilled conch omelet. Another specialty, for lunch or dinner, is their lobster-and-conch ceviche, which I had and it was quite good.

Ceviche (sometimes spelled seviche) is one of the more interesting ways to prepare seafood. Instead of cooking the fish (or shrimp, scallops, lobster, or conch, etc.), it is marinated raw in lime juice, for anywhere from several hours to overnight, so that it takes on a "cooked" consistency and appearance. When mixed with onions, peppers, and tomatoes, ceviche is

The Florida Keys: How One Man's Crazy Dream Opened the Keys to Everyone

Standard Oil Company co-founder and railroad and hotel magnate Henry Flagler was 75 years old in 1905 when he began construction to extend his Florida East Coast Railroad beyond the southern reaches of Florida's mainland. It was an idea that nearly everyone told him was pure lunacy. What could be more preposterous than building a railroad that would hopscotch across tiny coral islands and over water for more than a hundred miles? But Flagler was interested in what he knew would be dramatically increased shipping traffic once a new canal, to be dug across Panama, was completed. His railroad would make Key West the nearest rail terminal to the canal, by 300 miles. It took 7 years to complete, four longer than first estimated, but on January 22, 1912, the first official train arrived in Key West, with 82-year-old Henry Flagler aboard. Fifteen months later he died. Arguably, Flagler's "Over the Sea Railway" still stands today as Florida's most astounding engineering feat.

The Florida Keys are a remarkable and scenic 100-mile-long string of islands that protrude from the top of the only living coral reef in the continental United States. They are connected by one road, US 1, which ends at Key West. Native-born residents in the Keys call themselves "Conchs." The term dates back to the arrival of the Upper Keys' early pioneers, who came from the Bahamas. In the 1780s many British Loyalists who had fled the United States following the American Revolution settled in the Abacos, the northernmost of the Bahamian out-islands. In the mid-1800s descendants of these Loyalists sailed from there to Upper Matecumbe (Islamorada), in the Upper Keys, and resettled. They were quiet and simple-living people who built their homes from driftwood, planted pineapple and key lime groves, and fished. Conch, a large shellfish plentiful in these waters (sort of Florida's answer to California's abalone), was a staple in their diet, and the nickname stuck. Eventually the name evolved to include anyone born in the Florida Keys.   (continued)

> Conchs like to think that the Keys are really an independent principality. In 1982 Key West attempted to be just that, when they declared secession and adopted the name "Conch Republic" following protest after a Federal drug-search roadblock that jammed all traffic to and from the islands for a week.
>
> With fishing and tourism the staple industries, it's no surprise that some of the best seafood in Florida can be found here. I've often heard it said that a mediocre restaurant in the Keys won't last a month because there's just too much good competition.

very flavorful and refreshing, as was my lobster-and-conch ceviche at Key Largo Conch House. Ceviche is thought to have originated in Peru but is served often in Spanish restaurants and in Central and South American restaurants. You'll find a terrific recipe for conch ceviche, from Phil de Montmollin, in the recipes section of this book.

Conchs that live in Florida's waters are a protected species, so restaurants usually get them from suppliers in the Bahamas or from down in the Caribbean.

Mrs. Mac's Kitchen, 99336 Overseas Highway, Key Largo 33037; (305) 451-3722; mrsmacskitchen.com. Many Key Largo visitors (and locals) consider it mandatory to start their day with breakfast at Mrs. Mac's Kitchen. There is a second location, Mrs. Mac's II, which opened in 2012, just down the road, but only the original serves breakfast. Jeff MacFarland opened Mrs. Mac's in 1976 and named it for his mother. Many of the items on the menu are her recipes. The original Mrs. Mac's Kitchen occupies a 1947 Conch-cottage-style diner alongside US Highway 1/A1A that was originally Grainger's Gulf Side Inn. In 1988 Angie and Paula Wittke, two sisters who worked for MacFarland, bought Mrs. Mac's from him when he decided to move up to Vero Beach. The small front room has a counter in the middle surrounded by bar stools, with booths along the windows. Pictures of regulars, famous and otherwise, grace the walls. Beer bottles precariously line the tops of the ceiling rafters. There is a perpetual 1970s–'80s soundtrack playing. Journey's "Any Way You Want It" was playing when I ordered. So when I asked the waitress how they prepared the mahi in the fish-and-grits, she replied without missing a beat, "Any way you want it."

You could come here for the character alone, but lucky for us, the food is fantastic. Grits and Grunt (a lesser cousin to the snapper) is a traditional Keys fisherman's and scuba diver's breakfast. Mrs. Mac's version substitutes mahi for grunt, and they just call it fish-and-grits. I ordered my mahi the way I wanted it, grilled. It was fresh off the boat and a perfect complement to the steaming bowl of grits. They have a killer key lime pie here too. Sure, you can have key lime pie for breakfast. They also have lobster-and-grits and a crab cake eggs Benedict. Plus they are open for lunch and dinner (as is Mrs. Mac's II) and serve some tantalizing entrees like whole yellowtail snapper scored and deep-fried.

Sundowners, 103900 Overseas Highway, Key Largo 33037; (305) 451-4502; sundownerskeylargo.com. Sundowners owner and chef Bobby Stoky grew up fishing and diving around Key Largo when he wasn't working in the kitchen at his family's Señor Frijoles Mexican Restaurant. In 1985 Bobby's family opened Sundowners next door to Señor Frijoles. Bobby now owns and runs both, along with Ballyhoo's (see above) and Marker 88 in Islamorada. Sundowners' menu reflects Stoky's culinary diversity, with ambitious entrees like Portuguese pan roast with clams, pulled pork, chorizo sausage, and calamari; and seafood paella with shrimp, scallops, and mussels, and, get this, alligator sausage. Bobby's lobster bisque gets

high marks too, as does the Super-Jumbo Key West Pink Shrimp Cocktail, with big enough shrimp to nearly constitute a meal for me.

Key West

B.O.'s Fish Wagon, 801 Caroline Street, Key West 33040; (305) 294-9272; bosfishwagon.com. It's not "Bo's," it's "B.O.'s," for Bud Owen, the owner. Sometime around 1990 Bud started peddling his fish sandwiches out of a wagon, usually parked somewhere on Duval. Eventually it all just took root at the corner of Caroline and William Streets. From the outside it's hard to tell if this is a restaurant or the entrance to a junkyard. A circa-1940s pickup truck plastered with stickers shores up one side. The rest is 2-by-4s, corrugated tin, umbrellas, and crab trap floats. Chickens run wild underfoot, and there isn't a level spot of floor or a level table in the joint. But their conch fritters and their grouper sandwiches are much in demand. And they make killer homemade limeade.

Blackfin Bistro, 918 Duval Street, Key West 33040; (305) 509-7408; blackfinbistro.com. Michael and Joseph Castellano and Thomas Quartararo opened Blackfin Bistro right on Duval Street (down at Duval's quieter, south end) in 2009. This is Key West with an Italian twist. The lobster salad with pineapple, grapefruit, baby greens, and citrus vinaigrette makes a good starter. The steamed mussels and the shrimp Provençal are great standards that are always on the menu, but the Chef's "Catch of the Day" Seafood Linguini with shrimp and mussels in a cognac tomato cream sauce is a favorite. On my last visit I had their special Hogfish with Mango and Vanilla Cream Sauce, and it was out of this world.

Blue Heaven, 729 Thomas Street, Key West 33040; (305) 296-8666; blueheavenkw.com. If you want great seafood for breakfast in Key West, then Blue Heaven, in the Historic Bahamian Village District of Old Town, is the place to go. Actually, same goes for lunch and dinner, but don't expect to make a reservation. Unless you have a large party, they won't take a reservation. And forget driving here. There's no parking. Walk, bicycle, or take a taxi. You'll wait a half hour to get a table, but it's worth it. The century-old Conch house and attached outbuildings at the corner of Thomas and Petronia Streets contain Blue Heaven's kitchen, offices, and gift shop, but the restaurant seating is entirely outdoors, in the backyard. Yes, you may be subject to changing weather. In the summer it rains every afternoon in the Keys, although at Blue Heaven you will be somewhat protected by a giant kapok tree canopy, umbrellas, and old sailboat sails strung overhead. When Richard Hatch and Suann Kitchar first opened it in 1992, they called it Ricky's Blue Heaven, but after Jimmy Buffet wrote *Blue Heaven Rendezvous* a couple years later, the shortened version stuck. This location has some colorful history. It seems it was a genuine monument to bad behavior. It was a bordello, a cockfighting arena, and a boxing ring (called the Blue Goose) where locals wagered on fights, and reportedly Ernest Hemingway occasionally boxed and refereed. Remnants of those days remain. The presumed descendants of the fighting roosters still scurry around under the tables, chased by an occasional cat.

On most "Best Key West Restaurants" lists (including mine), Blue Heaven shares top billing with Louie's Backyard. For breakfast or brunch try the lobster eggs Benedict or the outrageously delicious shrimp-and-grits, with Key West pinks and grits mixed with white-wine butter, scallions, and cheese. And be sure to ask for some of their fresh-baked, light,

Key West: From Wreckers to Writers

Key West is, quite literally, the end of the road. It's as far south as you can get and still be in Florida, or in the United States for that matter. One of Key West's most popular tourist photo spots is alongside the US Highway 1 "Mile Marker 0" sign.

It's true that Key West is the westernmost, as well as the southernmost, of the Florida Keys, but the name actually comes from a mispronunciation of *Cayo Hueso*, which is Spanish for "Island of Bones." In the 1700s Spanish fishermen reported finding piles of human bones on the island's shore, likely the remains of a band of Calusa Indians who lost a battle to either Tequesta or Carib Indians, it's uncertain which.

By the early 1800s Key West had a lucrative and burgeoning industry: salvaging the cargoes of ships smashed on the outlying reefs. It was called "wrecking" and was extremely dangerous work, with a high mortality rate, but brave Key Westers could make a healthy living at it. Typically a wrecker would retain at least half the value of the cargo. Most of Key West's "wreckers" were transient from the Bahamas and Cuba, but following the War of 1812, some small groups of New Englanders from Connecticut and Rhode Island came and settled permanently in Key West. In 1828 the United States courts stepped in to regulate what some considered a dubious industry. Wreckers and their ships had to be licensed. A maritime court, established in Key West, decided how

fluffy, and sweet on the inside, crunchy on the outside banana bread. For dinner main courses go for the yellowtail snapper, sautéed with citrus beurre blanc over capellini, or the garlic and jerk seared barbecued shrimp simmered in Red Stripe Beer. Finish it off with a towering slice of key lime pie. Call me a heretic, but I like meringue on my key lime pie, and Blue Heaven has the best I've tried in Key West.

Conch Republic Seafood Company, 631 Greene Street, Key West 33040; (305) 294-4403; conchrepublicseafood.com. Conch Republic, in Key West's "Bight" historic commercial-fishing dock district, was originally a sponge-processing warehouse and market. Sponge diving was big here

the proceeds of salvages were disbursed. This did not, however, stifle the wrecking industry. In fact, this was the beginning of Key West's golden era. From the 1830s through the 1840s, Key West may have been the richest per-capita city in the United States. But it would not last forever. In the 1850s the US government began erecting lighthouses along the reefs in the Keys in an effort to prevent shipwrecks, which they did, and the industry evaporated. The Wrecking License Bureau finally closed in 1921.

Key West has long attracted creative folks, artists, and writers, among them John Audubon, Tennessee Williams, Robert Frost, and Key West's most famous resident writer, Ernest Hemingway, who lived on the island from 1928 to 1940. Between afternoon fishing expeditions and all-night bar expeditions, he produced some of his best-known work, including *A Farewell to Arms* and *To Have and Have Not*.

Ever resilient, Key West has managed to reinvent itself time and again. Sponging, cigar making, fishing, tourism, even treasure hunting, have all been industries that have kept the island afloat. Today Key West is an odd mix of tacky tourism and well-preserved history. And many of the creative folks making waves here now are chefs and restaurant owners. Key West has become renowned for its restaurants, where outstanding seafood can be found at both ramshackle dives like B.O.'s Fish Wagon and gourmet 5-star eateries like Louie's Backyard.

until around 1905–10 when the sponge diving industry focus shifted north to Tarpon Springs. After sponging, the building became Singleton Fish House and included Key West's largest ice plant. In the early 1990s this area began to see restaurants and other tourist-related businesses pop up, and one of the first was Conch Republic. Some of their specialties are: seared coriander-spiced tuna steak, baked oysters callaloo (a leafy Caribbean green, also called amaranth), cracked conch, and blackened Key West pink shrimp in a Cuban sofrito (tomatoes, garlic, olive oil, and onions) sauce. They did their peel-and-eat shrimp with royal reds the last time I was there. Royal reds are deepwater shrimp that have a little sweeter, almost lobster-like flavor.

Half Shell Raw Bar, 231 Margaret Street, Key West 33040; (305) 294-7496; halfshellrawbar.com. Like the image of Ernest Hemingway on Sloppy Joe's T-shirts, the Alberto Vargas–style polka-dot-bikinied pinup girl holding a platter of oysters on Half Shell Raw Bar's sign is a classic Key West icon. What had been a commercial shrimp-processing dock-front warehouse was converted in 1972 into a bar that served fresh-shucked oysters. Most of Half Shell's original customers were fishermen and dockworkers, and today they are mostly tourists, but the original business model worked and they've stuck with it. That same business model has been replicated at countless restaurants across Florida ever since, but Half Shell was the prototype. The menu has expanded considerably over the decades, however. The raw bar now includes Middle Neck clams and Key West pink steamed peel-and-eat shrimp. I've been eating a lot of peel-and-eat shrimp lately, to the point of possibly becoming an aficionado, and Half Shell's fresh Gulf Key West pinks, steamed in beer and Old Bay, are near the top of my list. Naturally, Half Shell's biggest seller is still fresh-shucked oysters on the half shell, and you can also get them broiled: Rockefeller, garlic cream (with tomatoes on top), or andouille (with sausage). Other starters and snacks include conch fritters, conch ceviche, crab fritters, and fried calamari. And besides fish-and-chips, shrimp-and-chips, and

oysters-and-chips platters, they offer some tantalizing specialties including crab-stuffed shrimp, crab-stuffed snapper, and a fried cracked-conch platter.

Louie's Backyard, 700 Waddell Avenue, Key West 33040; (305) 294-1061; louiesbackyard.com. In 1971 Louie and Frances Signorelli turned the waterfront backyard behind their house at the end of Waddell Avenue into a small restaurant. It is a historic house, built at the turn of the century by wealthy wrecker and ship captain James Randall Adams, but back then nobody cared about historic stuff, and Louie needed to make a living. What came to be known as Louie's Backyard had just a dozen tables, but the food was good and word-of-mouth traveled fast in backwater 1970s Key West. Thomas McGuane, Hunter Thompson, and Jimmy Buffet (back when they only played him on country stations) were regulars at Louie's. It closed for a while in the late 1970s, and then Pat Tenney and her husband, Phil, bought it and in 1983 renovated extensively, giving Louie's Backyard a rebirth. The menu and the atmosphere moved upscale, but Louie's truly came to the attention of the outside world when Norman Van Aken (now Florida's most

famous chef) came on board as head chef in 1985. It was Van Aken who hired Doug Shook. When Van Aken left, Shook took over as executive chef, which he still is today. Pat Tenney passed away in 2010, but Louie's Backyard is still owned and operated by Phil and their son Jed Tenney.

The food is exceptional, but it is the combination of food and atmosphere that makes Louie's such a magical place. There is a dog beach next door, and if you wish to visit Louie's with your four-legged companion, they have a side stairway so that people with dogs can go to the bar (but not the restaurant; sorry Fido). The Signorellis' backyard has expanded considerably through the decades and includes both that bar and outdoor dining tables, all with arguably the best view in Key West. Dine on some of Doug Shook's finest: Start with lobster braised in truffle butter with spinach and prosciutto, or grilled shrimp, octopus, and garlic sausage. For lunch I like the fish tacos with a spicy chipotle–sour cream sauce or the Maine lobster roll. For dinner try the porcini-crusted king salmon, the miso-glazed grilled yellowfin tuna (I've had that one more than once), or whatever the fresh catch is cooked however Chef Shook recommends.

Seven Fish, 632 Olivia Street, Key West 33040; (305) 296-2777; 7fish .com. Seven Fish opened in 1997 in an unassuming white 1-story building tucked away in the Old Town residential neighborhood. For a little while it was a locals' secret. From the outside you could drive by and easily miss it. I did last time, and I'd eaten there several times before. Other than

street-side, there is no parking, but you can park a few blocks away and walk. As of this writing, Seven Fish is constructing a new, larger location nearby, presumably with parking. It's scheduled to open in late 2016. The locals tried to keep this one to themselves because it's one of Key West's best.

At Seven Fish they like to grill fish. I had an outrageously good grilled black grouper last visit, and their seafood marinara pasta with grilled fresh-catch fish, clams, and shrimp is wonderful, but make sure you're hungry! They also do a terrific seafood ceviche appetizer, and if the fresh-catch-of-the-day special comes with their Thai yellow curry sauce, get it!

Marathon

Castaway Waterfront Restaurant, 1406 Ocean View Avenue, Marathon 33050; (305) 743-6247; jonesn4sushi.com. Castaway was almost as tricky to find as Keys Fisheries (see below), but at least there's a sign on the highway. Turn east on 15th Street and just wind around and follow the signs. John and Arlene Mirabella's Castaway Restaurant is the oldest operating restaurant on Marathon. It opened in 1951. In its early days it doubled as a bait shop and marina, but people came for the beer-steamed shrimp (and probably for the beer too). Today the atmosphere is as Keys-casual as it always was, but the menu has shifted upscale over the decades. It's Marathon's sushi go-to place now. I tried their Spicy Tuna Sandwich sushi. It came with masago (bright orange fish roe from capelin, a North Atlantic/Icelandic smelt) and sesame seeds, and instead of a traditional roll, it came quartered, like a sandwich. If you're not a sushi fan, no problem. Try hogfish stuffed with shrimp and scallops, or Snapper Mazatlán with artichoke hearts in a white wine cream basil sauce. Plus they have all the raw bar regulars: fresh-shucked oysters, Middle Neck clams, and yes, they still have Beer-Steamed Peel and Eat Shrimp.

Island Fish Company, 12648 Overseas Highway, Marathon 33050; (305) 743-4191; islandfishco.com. Island Fish Company is yet another thatched-roof tiki hut waterfront eatery, but that's what we come to the Keys for. And the food is terrific. Our Mango Blue Crab Cakes were chock-full of lump crab, peppers, and pieces of mango, then quick-seared in a pan. They served it with a tangy mustard–key lime sauce. They also have conch fritters, conch ceviche, and here's a new one: lobster egg rolls, and that's just starters. Their entrees lean toward Caribbean preparation: pan-seared grouper with pineapple salsa, dolphin (mahi) pico de gallo, and Key West pink shrimp stuffed with mango and crabmeat.

Keys Fisheries Market & Marina, 3502 Gulfview Avenue, Marathon 33050; (305) 743-4353; keysfisheries.com. Inexplicably there is no sign on US Highway 1/A1A to point you down the right road to Keys Fisheries. Just so you'll know, it's 35th Street. Turn west until you arrive at the water. Like their parent company, Joe's Stone Crab Restaurant in Miami Beach, they really don't need to advertise. Reputation and word-of-mouth brings in all the customers they can handle.

There's a marina here and the fish market, but most come for the restaurant. Order at the walk-up window, but remember to ask them what the "theme" of the day is. You see, nobody uses their real name to place an order. The theme could be anything that strikes the Keys Fisheries folks' mood that day: baseball players, movie stars, famous gangsters, dead baseball players, live baseball players, dead movie stars, live movie stars, and . . . well, just dead gangsters. Just pick a name and they'll call it when your order is up. I was Robert De Niro last time. "De Niro! Dinner's ready!" Robert De Niro got the grilled grouper sandwich, which was simply delicious. They put a little blackening seasoning on it, but other than that, they just let the "fresh out of the Atlantic that morning" fish do the talking. "Hey . . . You talkin' to me?" They've got lots of other choices as well: lobster sautéed, broiled, grilled, or lobster mac and cheese. They have mahi, snapper, hogfish, stone crab claws, conch, and shrimp; basically if it swims in these waters, they serve it. Roberta De Niro (actually Nancy Pepper) had the fried mahi tacos and they were spot-on too. We carried our baskets to one of the dockside park benches where we could toss a few spare french fries over the side to tarpon schooling in the water next to us.

Ramrod Key

Boondocks Grille and Miniature Golf, 27205 Overseas Highway, Ramrod Key 33042; (305) 872-4094; boondocksus.com. Don't let the Miniature Goony Golf sign fool you. Boondocks serves outstanding, very fresh seafood. On my pals' annual June fishing-and-scuba expedition, we always stop at Boondocks on the way down for early dinner because it's so good. On this year's trip I had the hogfish char-grilled with lemon-pepper seasoning. We also got a couple orders of conch fritters for the table, plus some of Boondocks's scrumptious Roasted Corn Lobster Cakes. The rest of the gang ordered yellowtail snapper, tripletail (one of my favorites), swordfish, and wahoo, none of which any of them would let me sample. I have yet to play goony golf at Doundocks, but then again I don't come to the Keys to play golf.

Stock Island

Hogfish Bar & Grill, 6810 Front Street, Stock Island 33040; (305) 293-4041; hogfishbar.com. Stock Island is the next island north of Key West, just across the bridge. It's mostly industrial: boat repair, marinas, commercial fishing operations, and other businesses that serve Key West's tourist industry. And then there's the Hogfish Bar & Grill, one of Key West's most popular restaurants, and it's not actually on Key West. On my most recent fishing-expedition trip, we all dined at Hogfish one evening. Among our group of 10, we sampled jerk yellowtail snapper, grouper Reuben sandwiches, garlic shrimp scampi, blackened tuna tacos, shrimp quesadillas, and fried grouper cheeks. I had the grilled hogfish sandwich topped with cheese and mushrooms. So what exactly is a hogfish? It's in the snapper family (and tastes very snapper-like, which is good) and has a distinctive porcine-like snout, hence the name.

In 2010 Bobby Mongelli opened Hogfish Bar & Grill at this old fishermen's bar wedged in between boat-repair shops and docks, at Safe Harbor Marina on Stock Island. Mongelli is a classic self-made entrepreneur who got his start washing dishes at the Casa Marina Hotel in Key West in 1979. Today Hogfish seats over a hundred customers, and, despite its off–Key West location, is packed every night.

Sugarloaf Key

Mangrove Mama's, 19991 Overseas Highway, Sugarloaf Key 33042; (305) 745-3030; mangrovemamasrestaurant.com. Mangrove Mama's, on Upper Sugarloaf between Sugarloaf and Cudjoe Keys, reminds me of a Mrs. Mac's Kitchen-south, although Upper Sugarloaf is far less populated than Key Largo. The circa-1910 house was originally a railroad stopover station, part of Henry Flagler's Overseas Railway. It had a second life as a gas station and grocery store for years until 1979 when Tennesseans Gary and Nancy Bell bought it and opened a little breakfast diner. It didn't have a name, but Gary had no better place to park his fishing boat, named *Mangrove Mama*, than out front, so locals just started calling the

place Mangrove Mama's. The Bells moved back to Tennessee in 1988, and subsequent owners remodeled, adding an outdoor dining area. They still serve breakfast, lunch, and dinner, and they are known almost as much for their pizza as for their seafood. But how about this for seafood: coconut-encrusted grouper with piña colada rum sauce, fried lobster Reuben sandwich, plantain-encrusted hogfish with banana rum sauce, fried cracked-conch sandwich, littleneck clams in white wine and butter sauce, or mahi eggs Benedict for breakfast? And if you insist on pizza, try the Blue Water Shrimp Alfredo Pizza.

Fort Lauderdale

Coconuts Waterfront Restaurant, 429 Seabreeze Boulevard, Fort Lauderdale 33316; (954) 525-2421; coconutsfortlauderdale.com. Sometimes it's best to let good fresh seafood stand on its own. That's certainly the case with Coconuts' lobster roll, which is made with lump lobster claw meat and just a hint of mayo, and nothing else. They put it on a traditional Maine-style bun, and mine came with deviled eggs. I think I could eat this for lunch every day for the rest of my life and not grow tired of it. A good lobster roll is something you can wake up in the middle of the night thinking about. I have.

Seafood Lover's Florida

Like many other Fort Lauderdale restaurants, Coconuts sits right on the Intracoastal Waterway, so customers who own a boat and wish to avoid the road traffic can arrive by water. When I was there, quite a few did just that. Coconuts' menu is not all seafood, but the seafood that they have is outstanding. Try the fish tacos or the jambalaya (I know it's sausage and chicken, but it's got shrimp in it too), or the sesame seared tuna salad, and I guarantee you will not miss with the lobster roll.

Rustic Inn, 4331 Anglers Avenue, Fort Lauderdale 33312; (954) 584-1637; arkrestaurants.com/rustic-inn-fort-lauderdale. The Rustic Inn is a classic Fort Lauderdale seafood restaurant, opened in 1955. See Rustic Inn listing in the Jupiter section, below, for more information.

SeaWatch on the Ocean, 6002 North Ocean Boulevard, Fort Lauderdale 33308; (954) 781-2200; seawatchontheocean.com. SeaWatch has been a Fort Lauderdale (or more accurately, Lauderdale-by-the-Sea) icon since opening in 1974. The rustic Bahamian-fishing lodge architecture structure sits elevated behind sea oat festooned sand dunes overlooking the Atlantic Ocean. That view is certainly part of the draw. And when it is cool enough, they open the swing-out windows and let the salty sea breeze blow through. The other draw is their selection of seafood dishes, some

unique, like triggerfish schnitzel with chili lime butter and chardonnay-dill sautéed orange roughy (a white flaky fish that tastes similar to snapper). I came for lunch and was looking for something refreshing, and the shrimp salad sandwich was just what I wanted. They make their shrimp salad with tiny bite-size bay shrimp tossed in a light mayonnaise-and-lemon dressing with fresh dill. They have some killer appetizers too: smoked salmon tartine with focaccia toast and capers; calamari fried with basil aioli and soy ginger-sesame-lime-cilantro sauces; and a Chilled Seafood Tower with Gulf shrimp, lump crabmeat, oysters, and clams.

Hollywood

Billy's Stone Crab Restaurant, 400 North Ocean Drive, Hollywood 33019; (954) 923-2300; crabs.com. From the floor-to-ceiling glass windows on Billy's Stone Crab's (no relation to the Billy's Stone Crab in St. Petersburg) second-floor dining room, I watched 80-foot yachts idle past on the Intracoastal Waterway. Not a bad way to pass the time. Yes, Billy's is famous for their stone crab claws, but I had just eaten lunch at Joe's (that other famous stone crab place, down south on Miami Beach),

so I went for something different. Yellowtail snapper was one of their fresh-catch-of-the-day specials, and I ordered mine simply grilled as a sandwich. Fresh is important to owner Bill Hershey, who got his start in the seafood market business years before opening the restaurant. As a nod to those origins, Billy's still has a small fish market downstairs on the restaurant's first floor. Regular fresh-catch dinner preparations include lightly battered and sautéed in lemon-butter-wine, blackened, Bretone (with mushrooms, capers, shallots, and crabmeat), Oscar, grilled or pan-seared Caribbean (with pineapple, papaya, mango, and cilantro), and macadamia crusted.

Homestead

Alabama Jack's, 58000 Card Sound Road, Homestead 33030; (305) 248-8741; facebook.com/pages/Alabama-Jacks-Key-Largo-FL/179175785438865. Most people who drive down to the Keys assume there is only one route between Homestead and Key Largo: US Highway 1. But there is a detour. It's longer, but if you're hungry for some conch fritters or blue crab cakes or a grilled fish sandwich, then it's a

detour worth taking. On the way out of Homestead, watch for Card Sound Road (Highway 997/905A) to veer off to your left. Follow it and enjoy the scenery and solitude for the next 12 miles. If you are heading back north from the Keys, turn right on 905 just north of Key Largo. Right at the base of the Card Sound Bridge, you will find the quintessential backwater-Florida open-air dive bar and grill, called Alabama Jack's. Don't be scared off by the rustic appearance. Yep, it's a popular biker hangout, but the food's good and the folks that run it are friendly.

The old barge has been here since 1947, and it became Alabama Jack's sometime between then and 1953, depending on which history book you read. Apparently "Alabama" Jack Stratham was actually from Georgia, and he was a construction worker who reportedly worked on the Empire State Building. Somebody in a construction crew mistook his accent (yes, there is a difference between Alabama and Georgia accents) and the nickname stuck. After Stratham died in 1977, Alabama Jack's changed hands a couple times, and in 1981 Phyllis Sague bought it. Now her son and daughter Mike Sague and Raquel Dickson run it.

Conch fritters have been a longtime Alabama Jack's specialty, and their grilled mahi is a favorite of mine. Last time I was here, I had it in their tacos. They also offer steamed peel-and-eat shrimp, crab cakes, conch salad, smoked fish (whatever is fresh that day), and a spicy conch chowder.

Jupiter

Guanabanas, 960 North Highway A1A, Jupiter 33477; (561) 747-8878; guanabanas.com. If Gilligan's Island had a restaurant, this is probably what it would look like. Tables are nestled among dense jungle foliage with thatched-roof covering, which shades the outdoor seating well enough to be comfortable most of the year. Guanabanas's centerpiece is a large banyan tree, surrounded by the bar. It all backs up to docks on a tributary of the Loxahatchee River. Many patrons arrive by boat. It was just a little sandwich shop when it opened in 2004, but in 2008 they rebuilt it into the full tropical-setting restaurant that it is today.

Seafood dominates Guanabanas's menu, and they are a Fresh from Florida campaign participant, so all their seafood is guaranteed fresh off the docks and Florida sourced. Each day they list their fresh catches, prepared blackened with tequila-lime sauce, macadamia and coconut encrusted, potato chip encrusted, or lemon-butter pan-fried in cornmeal breading. Additional regular items include various shrimp and crab cake

dishes. I had a refreshing blackened shrimp salad with candied pecans, strawberries, and blueberry thyme vinaigrette dressing.

By the way, *guanabana* is a Spanish word for a cone-shaped and spiny fruit called sour sops, introduced to Spanish explorers by Florida's Taino Indians.

Jetty's, 1075 North Highway A1A, Jupiter 33477; (561) 743-8166; jettysjupiter.com. Palm Beach–area restaurateur Jim Taube opened Jetty's in 1992. Their elegant but comfortable dining room spills out onto an expansive waterfront deck with a scenic view of the historic Jupiter Lighthouse just across Jupiter Inlet. Jetty's specialties include char-grilled Hawaiian mahi, salmon Oscar, oriental barbecued swordfish, and sautéed yellowtail snapper.

Rustic Inn, 1065 North Highway A1A, Jupiter 33477; (561) 320-9130; arkrestaurants.com/rustic-inn-jupiter. Right next door to Jetty's, Rustic Inn has the same spectacular Jupiter Inlet and Jupiter Lighthouse view from their back deck. The original Rustic Inn opened in Fort Lauderdale in 1955, and the Jupiter restaurant opened in 2014. Founder Henry Oreal

came to Fort Lauderdale from Philadelphia in 1955 and bought an Italian restaurant, which he and his brother-in-law Wayne McDonald remodeled into the Rustic Inn. In 2014 Oreal, now in his 90s, sold the restaurant to Ark Restaurants Corporation. Garlic blue crabs were a specialty from the start, and naturally, crabs still feature prominently on the menu today. You'll find Maryland-style crab cakes, stone crabs (in season), Alaskan king crab legs, and garlic Dungeness crab, in addition to the garlic blue crab. There are other seafood offerings as well, including mahi, swordfish, flounder, and scallops, but I wanted crab. So I tried a Rustic Inn summer specialty: Summer Crab Stack, with jumbo lump crabmeat piled on top of pineapple and mango salsa, all drizzled with sweet raspberry vinaigrette dressing, and I was not disappointed.

Schooners, 1001 North Highway A1A, Jupiter 33477; (561) 746-7558; schoonersjupiter.com. In 1984 chef Joe Rudy took an old gas station and convenience store just off A1A and converted it into Schooners Fish Market and Deli. But before long it had evolved into Schooners Raw Bar and Seafood Restaurant. Now he just calls it Schooners. They get all their fish fresh and whole and fillet it in-house. Schooners is known for its hearty soups and chowders: Fisherman's stew, Key West conch chowder, and New England clam chowder. But there's lots more here: crab cakes, calamari, clams casino, and cracked-conch bites for appetizers and fresh-catch-of-the-day entrees. I had a jumbo shrimp cocktail garnished with mango salsa that was perfect.

Miami & Miami Beach

Joe's Stone Crab, 11 Washington Avenue, Miami Beach 33139; (305) 673-0365; joesstonecrab.com. Perhaps no Miami restaurant, seafood or otherwise, is as legendary and iconic as Joe's Stone Crab in Miami Beach. Joseph and Jennie Weiss had emigrated from Hungary to New York, but Joseph's persistent asthma convinced them to move, with 6-year-old son Jesse in tow, to the warmer climes of Florida in 1913. They landed in Miami Beach, but as you can read in the sidebar, the Miami Beach of 1913 shared no resemblance with the one we know today. At first Joseph ran a small lunch counter at the local swimming pool. In 5 years the Weisses had saved enough to buy a tiny bungalow, where they lived and set up tables out back, turning their new home into a restaurant of sorts. They served mostly seafood (but no stone crabs, yet), and there were no other restaurants around, so what they simply called "Joe's" quickly became popular. In 1921 an aquarium went up at the south end of Miami Beach, and one day one of the aquarium scientists brought some live stone crabs into the restaurant. Joe and his cooks experimented with various ways to cook them and found that boiling and then chilling worked best. Back then they sold 5 claws for 75 cents. There may be some argument about who was the first to eat a stone crab claw, but nearly everyone agrees, Joe's was the first to serve it in a restaurant. And the rest, as they say, is history.

Joe's son Jesse Weiss gets credit for growing Joe's Stone Crab into the colossal business that it is now, and the Weiss family (four generations later) still owns and runs it today. Joe's now occupies half the

Creating a Resort City

A hundred years ago Miami Beach had virtually no beach at all. It was just a mosquito-plagued, mangrove-covered spit of land like most of the rest of Florida's southeast coast at that time. Locals called it the "Peninsula," which it was until 1924 when a storm washed away its thin sandbar connection to the mainland. Two New Jersey farmers were the first to attempt to put down roots here. John Lum tried to grow a coconut palm grove in the 1880s, but he eventually gave up. John Collins (who had originally loaned Lum money for his coconut palm grove) came in 1909 and managed to successfully plant bananas, avocados, and mangos.

In 1910 flamboyant promoter, inventor, and auto industry tycoon Carl Fisher bought a vacation house across the bay from the Peninsula. Two years later Fisher happened across John Collins, who by then had begun the construction of a bridge connecting the Peninsula to the mainland. He negotiated a deal to finance the completion of that bridge in exchange for some of Collins's property. Fisher had the grand idea to cut down the mangroves and dredge sand from the bottom of the bay to build a resort city. But he drastically underestimated the cost of dredging. To the bewilderment of friends and business associates, Fisher plowed forward nonetheless, clearing the land and laying out the city. He poured millions of dollars into the project, which, in 1915, was incorporated as Miami Beach. Fisher had built a golf course, a yacht basin, and the Lincoln Hotel, but it wasn't catching on. He even tried offering free lots to those who would build on them. World War I further stalled the town's development, but following its end, in 1919 Fisher decided to add horse stables and a polo field to try to attract the wealthy elite. This may have marked the turning point of what everyone, up until that point, had considered Fisher's colossal failure.

city block between Washington Avenue, Collins Court, and South Pointe Drive, plus a good bit of the parking between Collins Court and Collins Avenue. Famously, they do not take reservations. Two-hour dinner waits are the norm. Just put your name on the list with the maître d' and then go take a walk, or sit at the bar and watch for celebrities. Here's my best Joe's tip: Go for lunch instead of dinner and get there right at 11:30 when they open. Tip no. 2: Do get a side order of the hash browns. They will be the best you've ever eaten, and the "small" order is enough to split between four people. And the stone crabs? This is the food of the gods. Nothing is better in the seafood world. Of course, they're not 75 cents for 5 claws anymore. The price varies with the market. I paid $60 for 5 large claws, one of my more expensive book-research meals, and believe me it was worth every penny!

The stone crab is a unique commodity in the seafood world. The crab survives. Stone crab fishermen take only the single larger claw and return the live crabs to the sea, where they will grow a new claw. The claws are immediately boiled, then chilled. That keeps the meat from sticking to the shell, and it takes the iodine tinge out, leaving just the sweet crabmeat flavor in. Florida stone crabs can only be collected between October 15 and May 15, and the claw must be at least 2¾ inches long. If you see stone crabs in a market or at a restaurant outside of that season, you'll know that they're not really Florida stone crabs.

Monty's Raw Bar, 2550 South Bayshore Drive, Miami 33133; (305) 856-3992; montysrawbar.com. Monty's Raw Bar may not be on par with some of the top seafood restaurants in South Florida, but I wanted to come back here because this was the first place I ever ate conch fritters, back in 1979, and I wanted to see if they were as good as I remember. It was called Monty Trainer's back then, and it was *the* waterfront happy-hour hangout in Coconut Grove. Monty Trainer's has a typical Miami sordid past. It seems the original owner, Monty Trainer, may have hid the restaurant's substantial income from the IRS. And then the subsequent owner came under intense financial scrutiny as well. Monty's sits on Coconut Grove City–owned property, and the lease is, as of this writing, up in the air, so I don't know how long it will be around. But for now I needed to try those conch fritters. At first I thought I had stepped into a time machine. Had Monty's not changed one bit in 35 years? Here was the same tiki hut decor, with a thatched roof, wooden palm-frond-shaped paddle fans, and the same lacquered wooden tables and bench seats. Would the conch fritters be the same too?

So I ordered a basket, and yes! Monty's conch fritters are as good as my recollection, still stuffed with hunks of conch, diced pepper, and celery, and they still taste as good as they did when I first tried them in 1979. Monty Trainer, by the way, is still around, and very involved with the Coconut Grove Chamber of Commerce and the Coconut Grove Arts Festival.

Parkland

The Whale Raw Bar and Fish House, 7619 North State Road 7, Parkland 33073; (954) 345-9190; thewhalerawbar.com. The Whale, just outside of Boca Raton in Parkland, is Danielle Rosse's (see Oceans 234 in the Deerfield Beach section) seafood-themed sports bar, with a giant orca hanging from the ceiling. They offer a wide selection of fresh-from-the-sea entrees, including fried Ipswich (Massachusetts) clams, fish-and-chips, and fried oysters, plus 3 kinds of chowders: Bahamian conch, lobster bisque, and New England clam. But their real specialty is raw bar items: oysters, clams, and peel-and-eat shrimp, which I feasted on.

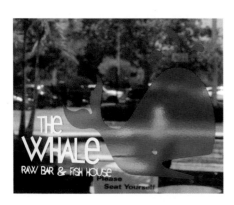

Pompano Beach

Fish Shack, 2002 Northeast 17th Avenue, Pompano Beach 33064; (954) 586-4105. You'll have to hunt around some to find this place, but it will be worth it. Mike and Elisa Focarazzo opened the Fish Shack in 2011, in a small neighborhood shopping cluster that it shares with a music shop, a coin laundry, and the Acts 2 Ministry Outreach Center. If you go for lunch, try to get there when they open at 11:30, because by 11:45 the 4 tables and 7 bar stools will be full. And by noon there will be a line outside. It's all word-of-mouth. They don't even have a website (and they don't need one). Raw oysters and Middle Neck clams are popular items, but I came for a heaping platter of the cracked conch. It comes fried, with a tangy honey-mustard dipping sauce. They also have conch salad and conch fritters, plus an assortment of fried platters including clams, oysters, scallops (the deep-sea variety), mahi, and grouper.

Is It a Bug, or Is It a Fish?

If you're a lobster lover and a bit squeamish, you may want to skip this sidebar. For those with stronger stomachs, here is a little seafood science: Technically, lobsters, shrimp, and crabs are phylumologically much more closely related to cockroaches than they are to fish, or even to shellfish (oysters, scallops, clams, etc.). Lobsters, shrimp, and crabs are arthropods, and more specifically, part of the subphylum of crustaceans, which means they have an exoskeleton and jointed legs, like their close cousins insects, arachnids (spiders), and myriapods (centipedes and other wiggly-crawlies). And just like those bugs, they also have open circulatory systems (no veins and arteries) and compound eyes.

Arthropods are the largest phylum of creatures on earth. There are plenty of subsets among them. For instance, the northern big-claw "Maine" lobster is quite different from the southern no-claw "Caribbean" spiny lobster, which is actually closer to the crawfish ("mudbugs" if you're from Louisiana). We routinely refer to their outer part as a shell, but it's actually not. It's a skeleton, and as these guys grow, they molt, which means they shed and grow a new one. That's where soft-shell crab comes from.

In 2011 researchers found a 480-million-year-old fossil of a 7-foot-long prehistoric lobster-like arthropod that they named *anomalocaridid*. Try fitting one of those on your grill!

In the Kitchen

The recipes that I've collected here have one main criterion in mind: simplicity. I wanted recipes that highlighted the seafood, not just what goes on it. Good fresh fish and shellfish have wonderful flavors all by themselves. Longtime friend Jeff Hammond's recipe for flash-fried fresh-caught mahi can be found below. It's his tried-and-true method for cooking a mess of fresh-caught fish for a bunch of people. I spend a week in the Keys every June, fishing with a group of friends including Jeff and the rest of the Hammond family. We troll offshore for dolphin (mahi) and bottom-fish for grouper. It's Jeff's job to cook each night (usually for 10 to 12 people) whatever we caught that day because he gets it perfect every time. Jeff insists that the secret to his consistency is keeping it simple and letting the flavor of the fish (not the seasoning) dominate. He explains, "Just a little tiny bit of sea salt actually helps bring out the flavor in fresh-caught fish, but just a little too much can destroy it." Another good friend, Michael Poole, gave me his recipe for smoked salmon (see below). It couldn't be simpler, but Michael's salmon is the very best I've ever tasted. I've also included a couple of "goes-well-with-seafood" items that don't contain seafood but complement it perfectly.

◆•• ————— ◆ ◆ ◆ ————— ••◆

Appetizers

Conch Seviche (Ceviche) 206

Cracked Conch 207

Cornmeal-Fried Florida Alligator Bites
   with Honey-Mustard Dipping Sauce 208

Swordfish Sliders 209

Blue Crab Fritters 210

Sweet Corn and Chorizo Sausage Stuffed Florida Clams 211

Italian Herb Shrimp Puffs 212

Camarones al Jerez (Shrimp in Sherry, Olive Oil, and Garlic) 212

Honey-Mustard Shrimp and Prosciutto 213

Main Courses

Cornbread Crab Cakes 214

Herb-Crusted Salmon with Jumbo Lump Mushroom Ragout 216

Flash-Fried Fresh-Caught Mahi (or Grouper) 217

Crispy Florida Snapper with Ratatouille 218

Grilled Florida Shrimp with Mango and Orange Barbecue Sauce 219

Easy Grilled Clams with Vinegar Dipping Sauce 220

Alder and Applewood Smoked Salmon 220

Sweet Cream Butter Broiled Florida Spiny Lobster Tails 221

Honey Orange Glazed Florida Grouper 221

Grilled Gator Kabobs 222

Grouper (or Merluza, or Snapper, or Trout) a la Rusa 223

Pompano Papillot 225

Sunshine Grouper 226

Shrimp and Swordfish Stew 227

Seafood Bisques

Grouper Thai Curry Bisque 228

Lobster Bisque 229

Perfect Complements to a Seafood Meal

Key Lime Pie 230

Corn Fritters 231

Conch Seviche (Ceviche)

Recipe courtesy of Phil de Montmollin, author of *Recipes from the Florida Keys: Lime Tree Bay Cookbook*, Anna Maria, Florida

SERVES 6

2–3 conchs
1 cup lime juice
¼ cup finely minced red onion
2 tablespoons finely chopped green pepper
2 tablespoons finely chopped sweet red pepper
½ cup olive oil
3 tablespoons orange juice
¼ teaspoon oregano
1 teaspoon salt
¼ teaspoon fresh-ground pepper
½ teaspoon Tabasco sauce
Lettuce leaf (for serving)

Clean conch well, trimming off all orange-colored flesh. Pound each piece with wooden mallet to tenderize. Dice very small (⅛–¼ inch). Cover with lime juice and let set, covered in the refrigerator, for 24 hours. Drain well. Add the remaining ingredients; mix well. Cover and refrigerate for 3–4 hours before serving. Check seasoning, to taste. Serve ¼-cup portions on individual plates with lettuce leaf.

Cracked Conch

Recipe courtesy of Phil de Montmollin, author of *Recipes from the Florida Keys: Lime Tree Bay Cookbook*, Anna Maria, Florida

SERVES 4

> 4–8 conchs, depending upon size
> ¾ cup lime juice
> 1 cup milk
> 2–3 dashes of Tabasco sauce
> 3 eggs, well beaten
> 1 tablespoon dried parsley flakes
> Salt and pepper to taste
> 1 cup flour
> Vegetable oil
> Lime wedges for serving

Clean conch well, trimming off all orange-colored flesh. Pound to tenderize and reduce thickness to ¼ inch. Place conch pieces in glass baking dish, pour in the lime juice, cover, and refrigerate overnight. Add milk and Tabasco sauce to eggs and stir well to blend. Mix dried parsley and salt and pepper with flour. Drain conch. Dip pieces in egg mixture and then dredge in seasoned flour. Fry over medium heat in small amount of vegetable oil until lightly browned on both sides. Serve with lime wedges.

Cornmeal-Fried Florida Alligator Bites with Honey-Mustard Dipping Sauce

Recipe courtesy of Justin Timineri, Culinary Ambassador and State Chef for the Florida Department of Agriculture and FreshFromFlorida.com

SERVES 4

For alligator bites:
4 cups cornmeal
2 cups buttermilk
1 pound Florida alligator nuggets

For honey-mustard dipping sauce:
6 tablespoons Florida honey
3 tablespoons Dijon mustard
2 tablespoons mayonnaise
1 tablespoon fresh parsley, chopped
Cayenne pepper to taste
Sea salt and fresh ground pepper to taste

To make the alligator bites: Preheat fryer to 350°F. Place cornmeal and buttermilk in separate bowls. Dip each alligator nugget into the cornmeal, then into the buttermilk. Let the buttermilk drain off slightly, and then dip the buttermilk-coated nugget back into the cornmeal. Lightly shake off any excess cornmeal. Place the coated nuggets into the fryer basket. Repeat the process until all the alligator nuggets are coated. Make sure not to overcrowd your fryer with too many nuggets. Cook the nuggets in the fryer for 2–3 minutes until they float and the meat is completely cooked. Take care not to overcook the alligator meat as it can become too chewy. Let the nuggets drain in the fryer basket, then transfer them to a plate lined with a paper towel.

To make the honey-mustard dipping sauce: In a mixing bowl, add all ingredients. Stir to combine. Taste and adjust seasoning with salt and pepper.

Swordfish Sliders

Recipe courtesy of Justin Timineri, Culinary Ambassador and State Chef for the Florida Department of Agriculture and FreshFromFlorida.com

SERVES 4

2 tablespoons low-fat mayonnaise
½ lemon, juiced
2 teaspoons blackened seasoning
4 3-ounce swordfish steaks, skinless
Oil for cooking
4 romaine lettuce leaves
1 large tomato, sliced
½ small red onion, sliced
4 small rolls, toasted
4 grape tomatoes, for garnish

In a small mixing bowl, combine mayonnaise, lemon juice, and 1 teaspoon of the blackened seasoning. Stir to combine, and store in the refrigerator until needed. Preheat a medium-size sauté pan over medium heat. Use 1 teaspoon of the blackened seasoning to season both sides of all 4 swordfish steaks. Add 1 tablespoon of oil to the preheated sauté pan. Carefully add the seasoned swordfish steaks to the sauté pan. Cook swordfish steaks for 2–3 minutes on both sides or until they are completely done. Remove swordfish steaks from pan and let them cool slightly on a paper towel. Make sliders by evenly layering the lettuce, tomato, and onion on each of the 4 rolls. Place the swordfish steaks on each of the buns and top with the mayonnaise sauce and roll top. Garnish each of the swordfish sliders with the grape tomatoes on a toothpick.

Blue Crab Fritters

Recipe courtesy of Justin Timineri, Culinary Ambassador and State Chef for the Florida Department of Agriculture and FreshFromFlorida.com

SERVES 6

½ cup self-rising cornmeal
½ cup self-rising flour
1 teaspoon baking powder
½ teaspoon seafood seasoning
Salt and pepper to taste
1 clove garlic, minced
1 medium onion, minced
¼ cup fresh parsley, minced
½ cup buttermilk
1 egg
1 teaspoon hot sauce
1 pound blue crab lump meat
Canola oil for frying

In a large bowl, stir together the dry ingredients; add the milk, egg, and hot sauce, mixing until smooth. Fold in the crab. Heat the oil in a heavy saucepan or deep fryer to 375°F. Drop tablespoonful-size scoops of the batter into the hot oil. Fry 2 to 3 minutes until golden brown, turning once if needed. Drain on paper towels. Serve hot.

Sweet Corn and Chorizo Sausage Stuffed Florida Clams

Recipe courtesy of Justin Timineri, Culinary Ambassador and State Chef for the Florida Department of Agriculture and FreshFromFlorida.com

SERVES 6

24–30 medium-size live clams, rinsed
Sea salt to taste
Oil for cooking
1 small onion, diced small
1 link chorizo sausage, diced small
1 red bell pepper, diced small
1 cup corn kernels
1 teaspoon chili powder
Fresh ground pepper to taste
1 cup yellow cornmeal
¼ cup jack cheese, shredded
¼ cup fresh cilantro, chopped
1 egg
¼ cup water

To prepare the clams: Fill a medium-size stockpot halfway with water. Place stockpot on the stove over medium-high heat and bring to a boil. Lightly salt the water in the stockpot. When a boil is reached, add the live clams to the pot. Cook the clams until they just start to open, and drain them in a colander; run cold water over them until they are cooled off. Discard any unopened clams. Let clams drain well and place them in the refrigerator until later.

For the stuffing: Preheat a medium sauté pan over medium heat. Add 1 teaspoon of oil to the preheated pan. Add the diced onions and chorizo sausage to the preheated pan. Cook the onions and chorizo until the onions are translucent and the chorizo is golden brown. Add the bell pepper, corn, and chili powder to the pan. Continue to cook for 2–3 minutes. Season the ingredients in the pan lightly with salt and pepper. Remove ingredients from heat and add them to a medium-size mixing bowl. To the mixing bowl, add cornmeal, cheese, cilantro, egg, and ¼ cup water. Mix ingredients thoroughly; add a little more water if necessary so the stuffing is moist. Preheat oven to 375°F. Remove cooked clams from the refrigerator. Open up each shell the rest of the way so they can be stuffed. Place an even amount of stuffing in each shell. Place stuffed shells on a baking dish. Place the baking dish of stuffed clams on the center rack of the oven. Bake clams for 7–12 minutes or until heated throughout. Remove clams from oven and serve immediately.

Italian Herb Shrimp Puffs

Recipe courtesy of Justin Timineri, Culinary Ambassador and State Chef for the Florida Department of Agriculture and FreshFromFlorida.com

SERVES 4

24 large shrimp, cooked and peeled
¼ cup prepared Italian dressing
1 sheet frozen puff pastry, thawed
Seafood sauce or creamy Italian dressing

Heat oven to 350°F. In a medium bowl, toss shrimp with Italian dressing to coat; set aside. Lightly grease a baking sheet or line with parchment paper. Unfold pastry sheet on a lightly floured surface; cut pastry into 24 1-inch-by-2-inch strips. Wrap each shrimp in a strip of puff pastry and press the seam to seal. Place on a baking sheet seam-side down. Bake 10–15 minutes until the puff pastry is golden brown. Serve with favorite seafood sauce or creamy Italian dressing.

Camarones al Jerez
(Shrimp in Sherry, Olive Oil, and Garlic)

Recipe courtesy of Chef Chris Fernandez, Red Mesa Restaurant, St. Petersburg, Florida

SERVES 2 AS AN APPETIZER

¼ cup olive oil
1½ pounds large shrimp peeled and deveined
2 tablespoons minced garlic
¼ cup chopped fresh parsley
½ cup dry sherry
½ cup soft unsalted butter
3 green onions sliced fine
Salt and pepper to taste
Cuban bread or French baguette

Heat the olive oil in a large skillet over medium heat. When hot, add the shrimp and sauté a couple minutes, shaking the pan to cook evenly. Add the garlic and parsley and cook a few minutes longer. Add the sherry and reduce by half. Finish the dish by swirling in the butter and green onions. Salt and pepper to taste. Serve on sliced Cuban bread or French baguette.

Honey-Mustard Shrimp and Prosciutto

Recipe courtesy of Justin Timineri, Culinary Ambassador and State Chef for the Florida Department of Agriculture and FreshFromFlorida.com

SERVES 4

For honey-mustard-coated shrimp and prosciutto:
½ cup Dijon mustard
4 tablespoons honey
2 tablespoons soy sauce
6 slices prosciutto
16 large shrimp, cooked, peeled, tail on

For honey-mustard dipping sauce:
½ cup Dijon mustard
4 tablespoons honey
2 tablespoons peanut oil
4 tablespoons soy sauce

To prepare shrimp and prosciutto: Whisk together the mustard, honey, and soy sauce until well combined. On a cutting board, cut prosciutto into triangles; coat one side of meat with a thin layer of honey mustard mixture. Wrap prosciutto around center of each shrimp, leaving tail exposed. Place shrimp on a serving tray; cover and chill until ready to serve. Serve with honey-mustard sauce.

To prepare honey-mustard dipping sauce: Whisk together the mustard, honey, oil, and soy sauce until well combined.

Main Courses

Cornbread Crab Cakes
Recipe courtesy of Bruce Hunt, Tampa, Florida

MAKES 10 CRAB CAKES

For the crab cakes:
½ stalk celery
Olive oil
1–2 tablespoons mayonnaise
1–2 tablespoons spicy mustard
1 small (8.25-ounce) can cream corn
1 raw egg
1 3–4-inch square cornbread
½ lemon
Old Bay seasoning
1½ –2 lbs. crabmeat (½ of it jumbo lump, ½ regular lump)

For the sauce:
2–3 heaping tablespoons mayonnaise
2–3 heaping tablespoons spicy mustard
Juice from ½ lemon
Worcestershire sauce (about a dozen shakes)

Mixing the crab cakes: Very thinly slice the ½ stalk of celery and pan-sauté in a little olive oil until soft. In a separate mixing bowl, mix sautéed celery with 1–2 tablespoons mayonnaise, 1–2 tablespoons spicy mustard, the cream corn (drain off about ½ the cream liquid first), 1 raw egg, ½ the cornbread square (crumbled), juice squeezed from ½ a lemon, and Old Bay seasoning (to taste). Stir well, then add crabmeat (drain off liquid first). Gently fold crabmeat into mixture. Cover mix/bowl with cellophane and place in refrigerator for a couple hours.

Cooking the crab cakes: Form balls (by hand) about the size of a racquetball and set aside. Spread a little olive oil in a medium-high-heat frying pan. Place the balls in the pan and flatten slightly into patty. Sear crab patties (cakes) about 3 minutes on each side, just enough to get a little brown crust. Be very gentle when turning them over, or they'll fall apart. Remove cakes and place on an olive oil–smeared cookie pan. Drizzle more olive oil on top of cakes, shake a little more Old Bay on top, and crumble the remainder of the cornbread on top too. Place in preheated oven at 350°F for 12–15 minutes, or until outside gets a little brown and crispy.

Preparing the sauce: Mix 2–3 heaping tablespoons each of mayonnaise and spicy mustard with juice from ½ lemon and about a dozen shakes from the Worcestershire sauce bottle. Drizzle sauce over crab cakes.

Herb-Crusted Salmon with Jumbo Lump Mushroom Ragout

Recipe courtesy of Chef Harold Russell, Backfin Blue Cafe, Gulfport, Florida

SERVES 6

3 tablespoons butter
2 teaspoons chopped garlic
4 ounces white wine
½ teaspoon seasoning salt
8 ounces sliced mushrooms
1 pint heavy cream
1 beef bouillon cube
2 tablespoons corn starch dissolved in 3 ounces milk
2 (5-ounce) boxes croutons
2 tablespoons fresh tarragon
2 tablespoons fresh basil
2 tablespoons fresh sage
4 ounces melted butter
Dash of salt
6 8-ounce salmon fillets
1 pound jumbo lump crab

Preheat oven to 400°F.

To make the sauce: Melt 3 tablespoons butter and sauté garlic until golden brown over medium/high heat. Add white wine and seasoning salt, and sauté mushrooms briefly until just done. Remove mushrooms and add cream and bouillon, and bring to boil. Lower heat to medium, add corn starch/milk mixture, and allow to thicken. Add sautéed mushrooms back to sauce.

To make the crust: Coarse-crush croutons in food processor with herbs. Melt 4 ounces butter and moisten crumb mixture. Season with a dash of seasoning salt.

To make the salmon and crab: Bake salmon until just done (about 8 minutes). Remove from oven. Pat crumb mixture onto top of fillets. Top each crusted fillet with 2½ ounces crab. Return to oven until crust is brown (about 2 minutes). Top with sauce and serve.

Flash-Fried Fresh-Caught Mahi (or Grouper)

Recipe courtesy of Jeff Hammond, St. Pete Beach, Florida

SERVES VARIABLE NUMBER OF PEOPLE, DEPENDING ON HOW MANY FISH
CAUGHT

Fresh-caught mahi or grouper
Sea salt
Fresh-ground black peppercorn
McCormick Golden Dip Seafood Fry Mix
Natures Seasoning
Canola oil

Fillet and clean the fish. Then cut the fillets into 3-inch-square pieces and
spread on pan. Apply a very light layer of sea salt to one side of the fillets.
Do not oversalt. Then apply a light layer of fresh-ground black peppercorn.
Flip all the pieces and repeat. Mix McCormick Golden Dip Seafood Fry
Mix with some Natures Seasoning. Heat canola oil in fry daddy or kettle to
approximately 350°F. Lightly coat fish pieces in Seafood Fry Mix and drop
into fryer. Cook until you just begin to see them turn a light gold color, then
remove and place on paper towels. Watch closely. If they turn brown in the
fryer, you have overcooked them.

Crispy Florida Snapper with Ratatouille

Recipe courtesy of Justin Timineri, Culinary Ambassador and State Chef for the Florida Department of Agriculture and FreshFromFlorida.com

SERVES 4

2 tablespoons olive oil
1 onion, ½ inch medium dice
2 cloves garlic, thinly sliced
1 medium eggplant, ½ inch medium dice
2 medium zucchini, ½ inch medium dice
1 red bell pepper, ½ inch medium dice
1 yellow bell pepper, ½ inch medium dice
3 medium tomatoes, ½ inch medium dice
1 teaspoon fresh thyme, chopped
1 teaspoon fresh tarragon, chopped
1 teaspoon fresh oregano, chopped
Kosher salt
Freshly ground black pepper
⅓ cup olive oil
4 6-ounce red snapper fillets
1 cup all-purpose flour

Heat 2 tablespoons olive oil in a large saucepan over medium heat. Add onion and garlic; sauté 2 minutes until tender. Add eggplant and zucchini squash and sauté 4 minutes until slightly softened. Add bell peppers and cook for 2 minutes, stirring occasionally. Add tomatoes and herbs and reduce heat to low. Cover pan partially with a lid; simmer 20 minutes, stirring occasionally, until vegetables are tender. Season with salt and pepper to taste. Heat remaining olive oil in a large sauté pan over medium heat. Pat fillets dry and season both sides with salt and pepper. Dredge fillets in flour. Pan-fry 3–4 minutes each side until golden and cooked through. Serve fillets on a bed of the ratatouille.

Grilled Florida Shrimp with Mango and Orange Barbecue Sauce

Recipe courtesy of Justin Timineri, Culinary Ambassador and State Chef for the Florida Department of Agriculture and FreshFromFlorida.com

SERVES 2

½ cup orange juice
½ cup ketchup
1 lime, juiced
1 tablespoon soy sauce
Oil for cooking
1 bell pepper, diced small
1½ pounds shrimp, peeled and deveined
1 mango, peeled and diced
Sea salt to taste
Fresh-ground pepper to taste
¼ cup fresh chives or scallions, sliced small
Lemon and fresh parsley for garnish

In a small saucepan, combine orange juice, ketchup, lime juice, and soy sauce; heat until bubbly and thick. Preheat a large sauté pan over medium-high heat. Add 1 tablespoon of oil to the preheated sauté pan. Add diced bell peppers to the sauté pan and cook for 2 minutes. Add the shrimp and mango to the sauté pan and continue to cook for 3 minutes. Carefully add the orange barbecue sauce to the sauté pan with the shrimp. Continue to cook until the shrimp are almost done. Taste and adjust seasoning with salt and pepper. Toss in the scallion or chives and serve immediately. Garnish with lemon and fresh parsley.

Easy Grilled Clams with Vinegar Dipping Sauce

Recipe courtesy of Justin Timineri, Culinary Ambassador and State Chef for the Florida Department of Agriculture and FreshFromFlorida.com

SERVES 4

4 dozen littleneck clams, rinsed well

Vinegar sauce ingredients:
½ cup cider vinegar
1 teaspoon garlic, minced
½ cup green onions, finely chopped
1 teaspoon salt
1 teaspoon black pepper, fresh ground
¼ cup tomatoes, finely chopped

Place clams on grill about 4 inches from coals or gas flame. Close cover and roast for approximately 10 minutes or until clam shells open. Check every few minutes for clams that have popped open. Carefully remove the open clams to an aluminum pan, reserving juices in shell.

Vinegar sauce: Combine sauce ingredients in small bowl. Serve clams in shells with melted garlic butter or vinegar sauce.

Alder and Applewood Smoked Salmon

Recipe courtesy of Michael Poole, Winter Park, Florida

SERVES 8

Florida Sunshine Spice (ingredients are sea salt, orange-lemon-lime zest, ginger root, green peppercorns)
2 large (1–1½ pounds each) salmon fillets with skin on one side
Alder wood
Applewood

Sprinkle Florida Sunshine Spice liberally over salmon fillets (skin-side down) and smoke in smoker over mix of alder wood (¾) and applewood (¼). Smoke 40 minutes to an hour, depending on thickness of salmon.

Sweet Cream Butter Broiled Florida Spiny Lobster Tails

Recipe courtesy of Justin Timineri, Culinary Ambassador and State Chef for the Florida Department of Agriculture and FreshFromFlorida.com

SERVES 4

4 6–9-ounce spiny lobster tails, split open in the shell
¼ stick unsalted butter, softened at room temperature
Sea salt to taste
Fresh-ground pepper to taste

Preheat oven broiler on medium high. Place all 4 of the lobsters on a cookie sheet and make sure they are opened up down the middle. Evenly spread the softened butter over each of the lobster tails' meat. Lightly season each lobster tail with salt and pepper. Place lobsters in the oven on the middle rack under the broiler. Let lobster cook under the broiler for about 7 minutes or until just barely cooked throughout. Remove lobsters from oven and let cool slightly. Serve lobster tails warm with fresh lemon.

Honey Orange Glazed Florida Grouper

Recipe courtesy of Justin Timineri, Culinary Ambassador and State Chef for the Florida Department of Agriculture and FreshFromFlorida.com

SERVES 1

1 tablespoon honey
1 tablespoon orange marmalade
1 tablespoon orange juice
¾ teaspoon Dijon mustard
½ teaspoon light soy sauce
⅛ teaspoon ground white pepper
¾ pound grouper fillets

Preheat broiler. Combine all ingredients except grouper, mixing well. Place fillets on an oiled broiler pan and brush fillets with honey glaze to cover. Broil 5 to 6 inches from heat for 4–5 minutes until browned. Turn fillets, brush with honey glaze, and broil additional 5 minutes or until fish flakes easily.

Grilled Gator Kabobs

Recipe courtesy of Justin Timineri, Culinary Ambassador and State Chef for the Florida Department of Agriculture and FreshFromFlorida.com

SERVES 4

½ cup orange juice concentrate

¼ cup orange juice

2 tablespoons light soy sauce

2 tablespoons brown sugar

1 teaspoon cumin

¼ teaspoon cayenne

1 pound alligator meat, cut into 1-inch cubes

Assorted fresh vegetables or fruit, cubed (preparer's choice)

Wooden skewers

For the marinade, combine orange concentrate, orange juice, soy sauce, sugar, and spices in a medium glass bowl. Reserve half for basting. Add alligator cubes; stir to coat well. Marinate for at least 15 minutes or up to 2 hours in the refrigerator for increased flavor. Soak wooden skewers in water for 10 minutes to prevent them from burning. Thread marinated alligator cubes onto skewers, alternating with vegetable or fruit cubes. Heat the grill to high heat and grill kabobs for 6–8 minutes, turning once. Brush with extra marinade for the first 5 minutes.

Grouper (or Merluza, or Snapper, or Trout) a la Rusa

Recipe courtesy of the Columbia Restaurant, Tampa, Florida

SERVES 2

- 2 6-ounce grouper (or merluza, or snapper, or trout) fillets
- Garlic powder to taste
- Salt and pepper to taste
- 1 cup flour
- 2 eggs, beaten lightly
- 1 cup bread crumbs
- 1 stick butter
- 1 lemon, thinly sliced
- 1 hard-boiled egg, chopped
- ⅓ cup chopped parsley

Season fish fillets with garlic powder, salt, and pepper. Coat with flour. Dip in beaten eggs and coat with bread crumbs. Melt ½ stick of butter in heavy skillet over medium heat. When bubbly, pan-broil fillets until golden brown. Remove to platter. Melt remaining butter and pour over fillets. Arrange 3–4 slices of lemon on each fillet and garnish with chopped egg and parsley.

Seafood Shopping and Home Storing Tips

Here are some things to remember when buying seafood at your local market and storing it at home before cooking. My resource for this information is the Florida Department of Agriculture and FreshFromFlorida.com.

1) This first one might seem obvious, but it is important. Only buy seafood from reputable, commercial sources.
2) When shopping, buy your seafood last so that it stays colder. If you have a long drive home, see if your grocer will pack your seafood on ice for the trip.
3) Remember: Fresh fish, shucked oysters, and scallops should have a mild, sea breeze aroma. A strong fishy odor usually means they are not very fresh.
4) When purchasing live clams or oysters in their shells, test them by tapping the shells. They should open and snap back shut. If they are already open and stay open after tapping, then they are dead and should be discarded. Do not store live oysters or clams in sealed tight containers. Leave the container lid slightly ajar and do not refrigerate for longer than 5 days.
5) Buying fish whole is the best way to ensure that they are fresh. Look for a shiny outside surface with tightly adhering scales. Look for deep red or pink gills that are free of slime, and a clean, shiny belly cavity with no cuts or protruding bones. Again, they should have a mild, sea breeze aroma.
6) For fresh fillets, look for a translucent appearance, firm meat that is not separating, and sniff for that same mild, sea breeze aroma There should be no discoloration, and it should be packaged so that the fillets lay flat.
7) When storing fresh seafood at home, keep it in leak-proof containers for up to 2 days in the coldest part of your refrigerator.
8) Although I'm not a fan of frozen seafood, if you insist, freeze it for no more than 10 months.

Pompano Papillot

Recipe courtesy of the Columbia Restaurant, Tampa, Florida

SERVES 2

    1 onion, finely chopped
    ¼ pound butter
    1 cup flour
    2 cups boiled milk
    2 eggs
    Dash of nutmeg
    Dash of Tabasco sauce
    2 tablespoons sauterne
    ½ pound shrimp, peeled, deveined, and chopped
    ½ pound crawfish or lobster meat, chopped
    Buttered parchment paper
    2 large (or 4 small) pompano steaks, skinned

Sauté onion in melted butter for 5 minutes. Slowly add flour to form a roux. Let it cook dry, slowly. Add boiled milk and stir over medium heat to make thick cream sauce. Beat eggs with nutmeg, Tabasco sauce, and sauterne; fold into cream sauce. Add shrimp and crawfish (or lobster). On buttered parchment paper, spread ⅓ of the sauce and top with one slice of skinned pompano. Spread another ⅓ of the sauce, then another slice of pompano. Spread remaining sauce over top. Close paper over top; seal by folding edges together. Brush melted butter over paper and bake 20 minutes at 400°F.

Sunshine Grouper

Recipe courtesy of Phil de Montmollin, author of *Recipes from the Florida Keys: Lime Tree Bay Cookbook*, Anna Maria, Florida

SERVES 4

2 pounds grouper fillets
1 tablespoon lemon juice
¼ cup melted butter
3 tablespoons orange juice
1 tablespoon grated orange rind
Salt and pepper
Fresh-ground nutmeg
Chopped parsley

Preheat oven to 350°F. Place grouper fillets in well-buttered baking dish. Sprinkle with lemon juice and set aside. Mix melted butter, orange juice, and grated orange rind; pour evenly over grouper fillets. Liberally season with salt, pepper, and nutmeg. Bake for 15–20 minutes, depending upon thickness of fillets, or until fish flakes easily with a fork. Sprinkle with chopped parsley before serving.

Shrimp and Swordfish Stew

Recipe courtesy of Phil de Montmollin, author of *Recipes from the Florida Keys: Lime Tree Bay Cookbook*, Anna Maria, Florida

SERVES 6

¼ cup olive oil

2 cups chopped onion

2 cups chopped green pepper

2 cloves garlic, minced

2 (28-ounce) cans plum tomatoes

1 (6-ounce) can tomato paste

1 cup canned tomato juice

1 cup water

1½ tablespoons jerk seasoning

1 tablespoon sugar

Salt, to taste

1 pound swordfish steak, cut into 1-inch chunks

1½ pounds medium shrimp, peeled and deveined

Heat oil in large pot and sauté onion, green pepper, and garlic until soft. Crush the tomatoes by hand and add to the pot, along with the tomato paste, tomato juice, and water. Heat to slow simmer. Add jerk seasoning and sugar, stirring well to blend. Cover and simmer over low heat for 1 hour, stirring occasionally. Add more water if sauce becomes too thick. Consistency should be between thinness of chowder and thickness of pasta sauce. Check seasonings; add salt if needed. Add swordfish chunks, return to simmer, and cook for 15 more minutes. Add shrimp, return to simmer, and cook for another 3–4 minutes.

Grouper Thai Curry Bisque

Recipe courtesy of Justin Timineri, Culinary Ambassador and State Chef for the Florida Department of Agriculture and FreshFromFlorida.com

SERVES 6

- 4 tablespoons olive oil
- 4 6-ounce grouper fillets, cut into 1-inch pieces
- 5 cloves garlic, peeled and coarse chopped
- 1 cup shallots, thinly sliced
- 4 small dried red chiles
- 2 tablespoons fresh ginger, minced
- 1 large fennel bulb, cut into 1-inch pieces
- 1 cup carrots, cut into 1-inch pieces
- 1 tablespoon Thai green curry paste
- 1 cup unsweetened coconut milk
- 4 cups bottled clam juice or chicken broth
- Salt and pepper to taste
- 2 limes, juiced
- ½ cup fresh cilantro leaves, chopped for garnish

In a large soup pot, heat the oil over moderately high heat. Add grouper pieces and sauté until just browned. Remove from pan and set aside. Add the garlic cloves and shallots to the pan; cook over moderately high heat until softened, 3–5 minutes. Add the chiles, ginger, fennel, carrots, and curry paste. Cover and cook, stirring occasionally, until the vegetables begin to soften, about 5 minutes. Add the coconut milk and broth and bring to a boil. Cover and cook over low heat, stirring a few times, until the carrots are tender, about 10 minutes longer. Taste and adjust seasoning with salt and pepper. Add the grouper and lime juice; cover and simmer over low heat 5–7 minutes. Garnish with cilantro; serve hot.

Lobster Bisque

Recipe courtesy of Justin Timineri, Culinary Ambassador and State Chef for the Florida Department of Agriculture and FreshFromFlorida.com

SERVES 6

1½ pounds cooked spiny lobster meat
1 medium onion, finely chopped
1 rib celery, finely chopped
1 carrot, finely chopped
1 tomato, finely chopped
6 cloves garlic, chopped
2 tablespoons fresh tarragon leaves, chopped
2 tablespoons fresh thyme leaves, chopped
1 bay leaf
8 black peppercorns
2 tablespoons olive oil
½ cup brandy
½ cup dry sherry
4 cups fish stock or bottled clam juice
¼ cup tomato paste
½ cup heavy cream
1½ tablespoons cornstarch
2 tablespoons water
Salt and pepper to taste

Slice cooked lobster meat into medallions, reserving a few slices for garnish. Coarsely chop remaining slices; cover and chill. In a 6-quart stockpot, sauté the vegetables, garlic, herbs, and peppercorns in oil over medium-high heat until soft. Add the brandy and sherry; simmer until most of the liquid is evaporated. Add the fish stock and simmer uncovered for 1 hour, stirring occasionally. Strain the stock into a large saucepan; discard remaining solids. Add tomato paste and simmer for 10 minutes until stock is reduced to 3 cups of liquid. Stir in cream and simmer for an additional 5 minutes. Combine cornstarch and water in a small bowl and whisk into bisque. Simmer for 2 minutes, stirring, until slightly thickened. Add chopped lobster meat and simmer until lobster meat is heated through. Add salt and pepper. Serve garnished with reserved lobster medallions.

Perfect Complements to a Seafood Meal

Key Lime Pie

Recipe courtesy of Phil de Montmollin, author of *Recipes from the Florida Keys: Lime Tree Bay Cookbook*, Anna Maria, Florida

MAKES 1 PIE; SERVES 6 (OR 1 OR 2 IF YOU'RE REALLY HUNGRY!)

6 egg yolks
1 (15-ounce) can Eagle Brand sweetened condensed milk
½ cup key lime juice
1 graham cracker pie shell, baked and cooled
Whipped cream (optional)

Preheat oven to 325°F.

Combine egg yolks and sweetened condensed milk, mixing well with electric blender. Slowly add the lime juice, while continuing to mix until well blended. Total mixing time should be about 4 minutes.

Pour into pie shell and bake for 10 minutes.

Remove from oven and refrigerate for 2–3 hours or until set.

Serve plain or top with a thin layer of whipped cream.

Corn Fritters

Recipe courtesy of Dixie Crossroads Seafood Restaurant, Titusville, Florida

MAKES ABOUT 30 FRITTERS

Vegetable oil for deep frying
2 cups all-purpose flour
1 tablespoon baking powder
¼ cup granulated sugar
½ teaspoon salt
2 large eggs
1 cup milk
½ stick butter, melted
1 cup fresh corn
Confectioners' sugar, for sprinkling

In a deep skillet or kettle, heat 1½ inches of oil to 050°F over moderate heat. While oil is heating, sift flour, baking powder, granulated sugar, and salt together.

Whisk eggs, milk, and melted butter in a bowl until blended. Fold egg mixture and corn into flour mixture.

Line a shallow baking pan with paper towels. Drop tablespoons of batter into the hot oil. Cook fritters in batches small enough not to crowd. Cook about 5 minutes or until golden brown.

Place cooked fritters on baking pan. Sprinkle with confectioners' sugar and serve immediately.

Appendix A: Florida's Seafood Festivals

When you're surrounded by such abundance, there's always something delicious to celebrate or commemorate. Here are some regional gems.

January

Apalachicola Oyster Cook-Off, Apalachicola
3rd weekend in January
oystercookoff.com
The Apalachicola Oyster Cook-off began in 2010 to raise money for the Apalachicola Volunteer Fire Department. They have live blues concerts and a 2-day art auction, but the event's highlight is the oyster dish cooking contest on Saturday.

Florida Keys Seafood Festival, Key West
3rd weekend in January
fkcfa.org/seafood-festival1
This festival is put on by the Florida Keys Commercial Fishermen's Association and features live music, art, and marine-life exhibits, in addition to great seafood.

Goodland Mullet Festival, Goodland
The weekend before Super Bowl
goodland.com/buzzard.htm
The Goodland Mullet Festival is the quintessential local's all-weekend party. It was started by Stan Gober, who owned Stan's Idle Hour Bar. Stan passed away in 2012, but the party goes on. (See the Marco Island section for more.)

Key Largo Stone Crab and Seafood Festival, Key Largo
Last weekend in January
keylargoseafoodfestival.com
The Key Largo Stone Crab and Seafood Festival, Key Largo's largest festival, includes a raft race, fireworks, and live music performances.

February

Everglades Seafood Festival, Everglades City
2nd weekend in February
evergladesseafoodfestival.org
The Everglades City Seafood Festival is also a carnival, with rides, arts and crafts, and top-name country musician concerts.

Cortez Commercial Fishing Festival, Cortez
2nd weekend in February
cortez-fish.org/fishing-festival.html
This is a celebration of the historic Cortez fishing village's commercial fishing heritage and a great look at "old Florida."

Jupiter Seafood Festival, Jupiter
3rd weekend in February
jupiterseafoodfestival.net
Jupiter Seafood Festival features multiple top-name music acts each day, plus local restaurant booths serving their best seafood.

March

Original Marathon Seafood Festival, Marathon Key
2nd weekend in March
marathonseafoodfestival.com
The Original Marathon Seafood Festival began in 1976 and has grown into a major charity event that benefits local schools with scholarships.

Goodland Florida Lobsterfest, Goodland
2nd weekend in March
stansidlehour.net
Another Goodland party, this time celebrating lobsters.

Marco Island Seafood and Music Festival, Marco Island
3rd weekend in March
marcoislandseafoodfestival.com
This Marco Island festival began in 2009. It runs for 3 days and includes rides for kids, live music every day, and lots of seafood supplied by local restaurants and vendors.

Florida's Seafood Festivals

De Soto Seafood Festival, Palmetto

4th weekend in March

http://desotosff.com/

The Hernando de Soto Historical Society puts on this seafood and entertainment charity event, which began in 1986, in Palmetto.

Lionfish Festival, Naples

4th weekend in March

heightsfoundation.org/lionfish

The Lionfish Festival is put on by the Heights Foundation, a distressed-community rebuilding charity. Lionfish are an invasive species to the Gulf of Mexico, and the festival emphasizes removing them and cooking them. They are actually a quite tasty fish.

April

Sopchoppy Worm Gruntin' Festival, Sopchoppy

2nd weekend in April

wormgruntinfestival.com

The Sopchoppy Worm Gruntin' Festival celebrates the local practice of "gruntin' up worms" (for fishing). For more about that, see my St. Marks sidebar, "Gruntin' Worms."

Flora-Bama Lounge Interstate Mullet Toss, Perdido Key

Last full weekend in April

florabama.com

The Interstate Mullet Toss is a huge beach party that takes place around a contest to see who can throw a mullet the longest distance. See the Perdido Key chapter for more about this event.

Pompano Beach Seafood Festival, Pompano Beach

4th weekend in April

pompanobeachseafoodfestival.com

The Pompano Beach Seafood Festival is a music, arts-and-crafts, and seafood event that benefits local schools and other charities.

Halifax Oyster and Music Festival, Daytona

4th weekend in April

halifaxoysterfestival.com

This Daytona Beach festival started in 2009 to benefit local oyster-bed restoration efforts. They have live music and local seafood restaurant and food truck vendors.

Isle of Eight Flags Shrimp Festival, Fernandina Beach

Last weekend in April

shrimpfestival.com

The Isle of Eight Flags Shrimp Festival is one of Florida's oldest and longest-running—it started in 1963. Today it features a parade, a pirate invasion, live blues musicians, and naturally, lots of shrimp and other great seafood.

May

Panacea Blue Crab Festival, Panacea

1st weekend in May

bluecrabfest.com

The Panacea Blue Crab Festival started in 1975. There is live music and lots of seafood, but the main event is the Crab Pickin' Contest, where contestants crack and extract the meat from a basket of crabs. The picker with the most meat wins.

Palatka Blue Crab Festival, Palatka

Memorial Day weekend

bluecrabfestival.com

Yet another blue-crab festival! This one has arts-and-crafts exhibits and rock concerts each night.

June

Steinhatchee Scallopalooza, Steinhatchee

4th weekend in June

facebook.com/SteinhatcheeScallopalooza

Scallopalooza is a festival to celebrate Steinhatchee's favorite mollusk, the scallop. It benefits the local Marker One Community Outreach Program. Music, a live auction, and tasty fried bay scallops are the headliners.

August

Key West Lobsterfest, Key West

2nd weekend in August

keywestlobsterfest.com

This 4-day event kicks off the opening of lobster season down in the Keys. Lobster boils, concerts, and a street fair are the highlights of Lobsterfest; kind of like Key West on any weekend, just more of it!

Mount Dora Seafood Festival, Mount Dora

3rd weekend in August

mountdoramarket.com

Once a year Mount Dora fills up Evans Park with food trucks and booths with seafood, local fresh fruit and produce, as well as local artists' crafts and art.

September

Fiesta of Five Flags Pensacola Seafood Festival, Pensacola

4th weekend in September

fiestaoffiveflags.org/pensacola-seafood-festival

This 3-day festival started in 1977 and features nightly concerts and seafood served by some of the Panhandle's best restaurants.

October

Destin Seafood Festival, Destin

1st weekend in October

destinseafoodfestival.org

The Destin Seafood Festival also started in 1977. Local fish, shrimp, oysters, and crabs are served from food trucks and booths, and concerts are held each evening.

Cedar Key Seafood Festival, Cedar Key

2nd weekend in October

cedarkey.org/events.php

Local art and local seafood (particularly clams) are the Cedar Key Seafood Festival's big draws.

South Beach Seafood Fest, Miami Beach

3rd weekend in October

sobeseafoodfest.com/main

South Beach, Miami, restaurants show off their best seafood dishes at this one-day event in Lummus Park.

Frenchy's Stone Crab Weekend, Clearwater Beach

3rd weekend in October

stonecrabweekend.com

Frenchy's Stone Crab Weekend is a 2-day-long block party in Clearwater Beach, with great entertainment and stone crab claws fresh off Frenchy's own crab boats.

John's Pass Seafood Festival, Madeira Beach

3rd weekend in October

johnspass.com/index.php/seafood-festival

The John's Pass Seafood Festival on Madeira Beach has been providing great live entertainment and outstanding seafood since 1981.

St. Marks Stone Crab Festival, St. Marks

3rd weekend in October

stmarksstonecrabfest.com

The St. Marks Stone Crab Festival began in 1997 and celebrates the opening of stone crab season.

November

Florida Seafood Festival, Apalachicola

2nd weekend in November

floridaseafoodfestival.com

This is Apalachicola's other (and original) seafood festival. It started in 1964. Events include oyster-eating and -shucking contests, blue crab races, country-western concerts, and it all culminates with the Blessing of the Fleet.

Sponge Docks Seafood Festival, Tarpon Springs

2nd weekend in November

spongedocks.net/tarpon-springs-seafood-fest.htm

Tarpon Springs' seafood fest with a Greek flavor, featuring local art, music, and fresh seafood prepared Greek-style.

Appendix B: Florida's Seafood Seasons

When I interviewed Justin Timineri, the state of Florida's Official Culinary Ambassador, two of the things that he emphasized for home chef consumers were "fresh" and "local." He pointed out that an informed buyer (not just of seafood but also meats, vegetables, and fruits) can do a better job of creating a flavorful and healthy meal if they plan it around what is locally fresh and in season now. Justin directed me to their Florida Seafood Seasons chart (not to be confused with recreational fishing seasons) on FreshFromFlorida.com, and I've provided that information here (courtesy of FreshFromFlorida.com):

Alligator All year
Blue crab May through October
Clams All year
Flounder May through November
Grouper April through November
King mackerel January, May, and June
Mahi May and June
Mullet January, and September through December
Oysters All year
Pompano January through April
Shrimp May through December
Snapper (red) August through December
Snapper (yellowtail) March through June
Snapper (other) All year
Spanish mackerel January, February, November, December
Spiny lobster August through December
Stone crab claws January through April, October through December
Swordfish September through November
Tilapia All year
Tilefish January through October
Yellowfin tuna June through August

Index

Acknowledgments

Mary Lou Janson (my number-one contacts and recommendations person), Mandy Baca (one of my Mary Lou Janson connections, and Mandy recommended me for this book to her editor at Globe Pequot Press), Amy Lyons, Lynn Zelem, Tracee Groff, Nancy Pepper (who went to more than 30 restaurants on research expeditions with me), Justin Timineri, Phil de Montmollin, David Burns, Harold Russell, Chris Fernandez, Richard Gonzmart, Jon Gill, Dr. Cameron McNabb, Becky Dreisbach, Michael and Dr. Leslie Poole, Jeff Hammond, Mark Hammond, Keith Hammond, Betty Hammond, Ken and Marcia Wregg, Lee Hill, Kerry Bolio, Gary Katuin, Doug Davidson, Terrie Fleming, Holly Rush, Jennifer Tuohy, Paul Balthrop, Jim Burkett, Irene Maher, the Florida Department of Agriculture and Consumer Services/FreshFromFlorida.com, and the Florida Fish and Wildlife Conservation Commission.

About the Author

Award-winning writer, photographer, and third-generation native Floridian Bruce Hunt has authored nine books on Florida travel and history. In addition he has written and photographed hundreds of articles for magazines and newspapers over the last two decades. He spent five years as a regular feature writer and photographer for *DuPont Registry Tampa Bay* magazine. His work has also appeared in the *St. Petersburg Times (Tampa Bay Times)*, *Tampa Tribune*, and the magazines *Backpacker*, *Rock and Ice*, *Skydiving*, *Florida Trend*, and *Celebrity Car*, among others. He also writes the *Visiting Small-Town Florida* blog and the *Car and Diner* blog, and operates Bruce Hunt Images, a publishing industry–focused stock-photo website.